HOW TO CONNECT

WITH THE PEOPLE IN YOUR LIFE

By C J Kruse

Special Thanks

To my mom and dad – thank you for your love, patience, and belief in me. Thank you for being such exemplary role models. As I now raise two children of my own (and with a third on the way), I only hope that I can grow to resemble you both – even if only in part.

INTRODUCTION

In the modern era of portable, ever-present handheld entertainment, a revived focus has been given to the subject of connecting – not because connecting is a new need, but because it has become increasingly common for people to suffer the effects of having weak or sparse connections. A growing portion of the population now finds it common to feel lonely, socially awkward, or forgotten. A lot of people wish they were better at handling simple, everyday encounters.

Many of us, if you asked us, would say that we feel intimidated by common social situations, like getting onto an elevator with a stranger. Sitting next to an unfamiliar face at the company party. Bumping into a subordinate in the parking lot. We search for a simple understanding of to handling these situations, and wonder what we can do to feel more confident in them.

At times, maybe you've felt the same. You've wondered how to talk to your nephews and nieces when you're at your brother-in-law's barbecue. You've wondered how to reach out to your parents, who you feel you don't speak often enough with. You've wondered how to spark up a conversation with the person sitting next to you at the bus stop. Each of these situations require something from you – they require the skill of connecting.

But, a lot of us don't feel inclined in the area of connecting, and often end up doing nothing at all, or doing things that aren't very effective. Either way, the problem doesn't improve.

Perhaps, we try to impress others, hoping they will be drawn to us. Or, we may try to substitute quality for quantity, packing our lives full of meaningless connections and hoping our loneliness gets lost in the large numbers. But, none of these things help us.

This is because connection isn't about quantity; it's about quality. It's not about how many people we know; it's about how well we know them. And, how well they know us. It's also not about how cool, popular, or successful we are. In fact, it's not really even about us at all. Connecting has a lot more to do with other people – the way we treat, value, and perceive them.

If we want to matter to people, there may be only one rule; people have to matter.... to us. Maya Angelou may have summed it up best when she said, "*At the end of the day, people won't remember what you said or did, they will remember how you made them feel.*"

The most meaningful connections we experience aren't shared with celebrities or Nobel prize winners; they're shared with regular people, extraordinary perhaps only in one way – the way they make us feel important. Our goal in this book is to work towards building these truer, deeper connections. They are the kind that most dramatically enhance the quality of life.

While you'll learn a fair share about people skills here, this is not a bag of social tricks, teaching you to dazzle your way to the top, or a tutorial, telling you how to trick people into thinking you're the cream of the crop. You may find books like that out there, but this one is simply about learning to be a true connector. Period.

Here, we will talk about:

- Learning to break the ice with people.

- Learning to be a better conversationalist.

- Dealing with loneliness.

- Making/keeping friends.

- What it means to connect.

- The benefits of connecting.

- Common barriers and misconceptions about connecting.

- Different ways to connect.

- Connecting in difficult situations.

- Dealing with the pains of friendship.

- Coping with loss and rejection.

- Overcoming shyness

- Connecting with ourselves.

- Much, much more.

I have learned a lot on my own journey to become a better connector, and I would like to share it with you. I hope that you enjoy what you read, and that it benefits you on your own journey as well. There is a lot to talk about. So, let's begin.

CHAPTER 1

CONNECTION – A CLOSER LOOK

To start, let's talk about what connection is. What do you think of when you hear the word? Perhaps, you imagine two physical objects touching, such as a screwdriver connecting to a screw. Or, an electric socket, connecting to a wall outlet. Maybe you think of that old game, connect the dots, where you drew lines between points to form a shape of some kind.

Maybe you think of an old couple, sitting on a porch swing. Or, two old friends, laughing about old memories. Or, that stranger you saw at the bus stop – the one who made eye-contact with you and smiled. Any of these examples capture what connection is. But, none of them solely define it.

Because, connection isn't a precise recipe that we can follow from a cookbook. It is more of an artform than a science. Even when people seem to be going through all the right motions, we find that the right results don't always follow.

This is why we so commonly see people who are close, but not connected. Talking, but not engaged. Physically present, but emotionally absent. Sharing a bedroom, but still living in separate worlds. Surrounded by people, but still feeling lonely. Obviously, connection doesn't always fit into the small, logical box that we try to place it in.

For every rule we think we've found about connection, we seem to find an exception. There are plenty of people who seem to go their whole lives without much connection, and who seem to be just fine. And, there are those who seem to have connection at every turn, and who, somehow, still seem miserable.

Perhaps the best way to understand connection is to break it down into general truths and principles, and to look at them individually. Here are just a few:

- Connection is a noun – it is a bond. A relation. It is something that is invisible, but its effects can be seen.

- Connection is an action – it's what we do to bring things together. It is something that requires energy and effort on our parts.

- Connection is a skill. It can be learned. Sharpened. Mastered. Despite a person's current levels of proficiency, and despite any inclinations he was (or wasn't) born with.

- Connection is a necessity. It is something that we need – throughout all points in our lives.

- Connection is something that can be communicated, but it is not limited by words. It can be felt, sensed, or implied. It can be real or notional. Deep or superficial.

- Connection is universal. It is something that we are all wired to create and experience. Even if we don't know it. Even if we are shy, introverted, or think we are anti-social.

- Connection is an ongoing precondition. It exists as long as we do, and goes with us wherever we go.

- Connection is beneficial. When we have it, we are more likely to flourish. We are more likely to experience emotional stability and personal success.

- Connection is momentous. It can be given as a reward, or withheld as a form of punishment.

- Connection is a goal. It must be pursued. Fought for. Allowed into our comfort zones. Squeezed into our busy schedules. Given our full attention. Learned and relearned.

- Connection is one of the main points of our existence.

Do you agree with these statements?

Perhaps, we should look at the basic building blocks of connection. What are they? Since connection is the thing we are trying to build, it will help us to know more about the construction materials used to make it.

CHAPTER 2

WHAT RELATIONSHIPS NEED

There are a few crucial components that comprise every relationship. They are: effort, consistency, intention, and time.

A. Effort -

Relationships require effort. For most of us, the problem isn't a lack of desire. Rather, it is a lack of energy given to build great relationships. We simply aren't doing what we must in order to make them.

This work can include picking up the phone, driving to see a friend, lending a helping hand, or simply being a good listening ear.   It may not be hard work, but it is work nonetheless. If you skip it, you miss out on the results.

B. Consistency -

Consistency is another thing that relationships need, and it's what many of us lack. We tend to go long periods of time without calling or reaching out to the people we know. Then, we suddenly take notice of the distance that has formed and we scramble to make repairs. We pick up the phone and call people we haven't spoken to in ages, hoping that one small effort will erase the months and years of distance we've created.

However, this rarely works. Because, relationships aren't kept up with big one-time fixes. They're kept up with regular maintenance, sort of like a car. In our relationships, we have to make sure that not too much time goes by between oil changes, so to speak. This isn't to say that you shouldn't bother calling someone just because it's been a while since you've spoken; just that it's more ideal not to let yourself fall out of touch in the first place. Consistency always brings better results.

C. Intention -

Unlike when we were kids, many of us no longer have the means or the resources that we once made connecting easy. We no longer have tons of time. Nor do we see tons of familiar faces everywhere we go, the way we once used to at school. Now, if we want to keep up with people, it doesn't happen automatically; it takes intention.

These days, making plans feels like being thrown an extra ball while you are already juggling too many… a career, finances, a family life, and a never-ending list of house projects. With everything else going on, you have to be intentional to fit relationships in, or they will most likely fall by the wayside.

D. Time -

Time is an important part of connecting. It's the currency that we give in exchange for life's resources. At work, time is what you trade for money. At home, it's what you trade for progress in your chores or recreational activities. In relationships, time is what you trade... for connection.

All relationships take time to build. This is true for that old friendship you're trying to restore from the rubble, as well as that new one that you're trying to build from scratch. Time is what allows depth to form, and it allows common grounds to be discovered.

SECTION SUMMARY -

These are just a few of the fundamental elements that are most common in strong relationships. Also on this list, we might find kindness, empathy, thoughtfulness, and affection, among many others.

But, it may be even more important for us to notice what this list does not include. It doesn't include: tons of jibber jabber, loads of fake, plastered smiles, tons of facade maintenance, and tons of acting like a social butterfly. These are only things that we think we need in order to be more effective connectors, but they're actually quite unnecessary.

I say this because we often carry around some faulty notions about what we must do to improve our relationships. A large part of understanding what connection is, is understanding what it isn't. We will talk more about the common misconceptions we have about connection. For now though, let's consider something important!

SOMETHING TO CONSIDER -

As we prepare to go into more detail about how connections are made, there is something we should look at. That is, who we would like to connect with. And, to what degree. Because, it would be unrealistic for us to expect to have a deep bond with every person we come in contact with. Narrowing down our focus will help improve our aim.

As Zig Ziglar once said, "Aim for nothing, and you'll hit it every time." In other words, we shouldn't be vague about our goals. Do you know what you are aiming for? Which relationships in particular would you like to see strengthened? If you don't yet have an answer, that's okay. The point is to at least get you thinking.

Maybe you want to connect with that old friend from high school that you haven't talked to in ages. Or, your brother, who now lives in another state. Your parents, relatives, or acquaintances.

Maybe you simply want to be better at connecting in general. You'd like to feel closer to your coworkers, your neighbors, or those people at church who you always bump into but never know how to talk to. Or, you'd simply like to feel more comfortable relating with people. Any of these make great connection goals.

To help you narrow down your objectives, I suppose I should ask an even more fundamental question yet. That is: why? Why are these your goals? Does that question seem redundant? It's not. Let's talk a little bit about why.

STARTING WITH WHY -

Simon Sinek, author of *Start With Why*, said that "People don't buy what you do; they buy why you do what you do." In short, our motives matter – to us, and to others. Do you know what your own motives are?

Why are you interested in being closer to your brother-in-law? Or, why does that relationship in particular interest you more than others? Maybe, you know that he got fired from his job, and you would like to be there to comfort him. Maybe you want to spend more time with his kids. Any of these are great answers, but even they point to deeper "why" questions.

What explains your motivations? What makes you so interested in his kids? Are your motives purely altruistic? Are you doing all this because you want to be a part of your brother-in-law's tribe? Or, are you trying to impress your spouse by proving that you care about her family? Either way, it will be good for you to know why.

Similarly, why are you interested in deepening your connection with that coworker of yours? Is it simply because you think you could learn a lot from her professionally? Or, could your interests be romantic? Knowing your own motives will help guide your approach.

Our motives matter. And yet, that doesn't mean they always have to match the motives of those we are trying to connect with. Sometimes, even differing motives can lead to mutually satisfying relationships.

You want to get to know your nephew because he's fun and cool. But, he wants to get to know you because you're old enough to help him learn how to drive. Even though you want different things, you both have something to offer each other.

Connection is like an investment. A long-term investment, to be more precise. Think about whether or not the relationships you're investing in appreciate in value. Will your contributions be valued by the those you plan to invest in? You don't want to pour your precious time and energy into something that won't hold your investment.

Sometimes, it can be hard to figure out where to invest our time, effort, and energy. We are drawn to some people simply because they are cool, funny, attractive, or successful. But, this doesn't necessarily mean that *they* are the ones we should invest in. What if they don't even notice us or care about us? Why not invest in people who do?

If you're still unsure how to answer your "Who" and "Why" questions, then maybe we should talk a little bit more about the benefits that we stand to gain from connecting. That, we will do next.

CHAPTER 3

THE BENEFITS OF CONNECTION

While we've already mentioned quite a few benefits that come from connecting, there are definitely more. Add the following benefits to the list that we've already begun.

#1. Connection earns us influence.

Some of the top-selling books today are on the subject
of influence. It seems we all want to know how to bend
others to our way of thinking. Ironically, it seems that
none of us are quite as thrilled about being the ones
who do the bending. Few of us start out our days
wondering, "Gee, I wonder which habit, behavior, or
perspective I can change for someone else today?"

Because, it actually seems that when people tell us who
to vote for, how we should drive, or how we should raise
our kids, they are, in a way, asking something of us,
rather than telling us something. They are asking for our
compliance. They are asking for our agreement. They
are asking for us to compromise so that they'll have a
likeminded ally. This isn't the kind of thing we will do
for just anyone.

We tend to only pay that price with certain people. Which people? Those with whom we have a strong level of connection. Our capacity to influence or be influenced, in some ways, is a reflection of the type of bond we have with someone.

Consider how you might respond to a close friend who tells you that you should try a certain product or wear a certain brand of clothing. Chances are good that you'll listen. Chances are good that you'll consider what he says. You may even try the product out for no other reason than because he recommended it.

However, if a strange salesman were to call you at dinnertime, recommending the exact same thing, you'd feel annoyed. You'd feel as though your personal space was being violated. His influence would be of a negative kind. It would only persuade you in the direction he doesn't want you to go.

Most good salesmen know that influence is about connection. This is why they will attempt to build connection with their clients before ever giving them their pitch. It's why they'll often go golfing or do recreational things together first. They are working to build influence. A good salesman knows he is selling more than his product. He is selling himself.

Maybe you'd like to have more influence at home. When you talk, your spouse doesn't quite buy what you're selling. She rolls her eyes when you share a thought or an idea. Why? It's probably not because you haven't shared enough of your logic, or because you haven't crafted your sentences carefully enough. The real reason she is turned off by what you're saying is because the two of you aren't connected. Even though you live in the same house, share the same bed, cross the same paths, and breathe the same air, it doesn't guarantee that the bond between you is strong.

It could be that your most recent interactions haven't been positive and constructive. Perhaps you've been too focused lately on being heard, rather than letting your wife feel heard. Maybe, you've been focusing too much on proving that logic is on your side. The problem is that none of that matters until you are connected.

An amazing thing will happen when you instead focus on being a better listener – she will instinctively become more inclined to listen to you. She will feel loved and appreciated, which will inspire her to show her love and appreciation to you.

This isn't just about marriage either – the truth that applies here will also apply to nearly anyone you want to persuade – even that niece of yours who no one has been able to talk sense to lately. While she may be rebelling against her parents, her teachers, and her authorities, there is a chance that she will actually listen to you. That is, if you're the one who has taken a special interest in her life.

If you have a history of asking her about her artwork, complimenting her uniqueness, sending her birthday cards, or just making an effort to call her every now and then to ask her how her life is going, then you have set yourself up to be influential in her life. In fact, you may be the only adult in her life that she will care about listening to. But, it's only because you've done the work to prove that you care about your connection with her.

If you haven't worked to establish any kind of connection, then your message will almost certainly fall on deaf ears. It will be unsolicited. You'll sound exactly like every other authority figure in her life that she has intentionally tuned out. Do you want influence? Influence comes by being connected.

#2. Connection benefits others.

It is important to consider that one of the main barriers keeping us from connecting is our own fear. We are so often afraid of looking stupid. We are afraid of being rejected. We are afraid of investing in something that might not pan out. These fears keep us from putting the proper amount of effort forward.

It might help us to rise above this fear by realizing that other people are usually dealing with the exact same fears. They too are afraid of looking stupid. They too are afraid of rejection. They too are afraid that their investment won't pan out.

So, in order to help them (and ourselves), it would do us well to focus on relieving their fears, rather than our own. To focus on meeting their needs, rather than our own. Suddenly, we would find our own fears vanishing, because we would be caring more for them than we care about what they think of us.

Your own anxiety suddenly seems smaller once you start to empathize for another person with anxiety. You suddenly get less tongue-tied when you realize that another person is tongue-tied too. Amazingly, when we focus on benefitting others, it often ends up providing us with the same (or even greater) benefit.

Because, just as you need a friend, so does your neighbor. Just as you want a sense of community in your workplace, so does your coworker. Just as you'll benefit by having someone to call when you're lonely, so will your sister, mom, dad, aunt, or uncle.

Often, it's only easy for us to notice what we gain from our connections with people, and to miss all the ways that we add value to their lives. Never forget that others gain something by having your insight, creativity, humor, and presence in their lives as well. You have a contribution. So, contribute. You'll find that once you do, everybody wins.

#3. Connection demystifies intimidating people and situations.

Have you ever had a magic trick explained to you? What happened once you knew its secret? Chances are, it wasn't as mysterious or perplexing. This is because our minds don't know what to do with the unknown, but they do know what to do with something that's familiar.

Well, there is a lot of unknown in some of the social situations we face that can be daunting and intimidating. And, it can be cleared up the exact same way. Once we become familiar with people, they become easier for us to talk to and be around.

It might seem scary to talk to a room full of strangers, but it's fun to talk to a room full of friends. It might seem scary to sit down next to a creepy looking guy at a bus stop, but it's not creepy if you know that his name is Danny and that he is a single dad who is on his way to visit his elderly mother. What's the difference in all these situations? Connection.

#4. Connection adds value and purpose to our lives.

Not only does connection demystify frightening packages, it shows us what's inside them — human value. Because, every human being is valuable. Everyone has something beautiful and unique to offer. We get to experience that beauty and uniqueness at a much closer range if we have close relationships with them.

You could even say that this is what gives our lives purpose. As Pablo Picasso once said, "The meaning of life is to find your gift. The purpose of life is to give it away." In short, people are who we give our gifts to, whether our gift is time, affection, energy, productivity, or creativity. When we have close people in our lives, we tend to have a stronger sense of purpose. When we don't, our sense of purpose can dwindle.

#5. Connection establishes a sense of community.

The word community means: "a feeling of fellowship with others, as a result of sharing common attitudes, interests, and goals." In good communities, people have each other's backs. They pick each other up when one falls. They lend each other things and have a sense of faith in one another.

Obviously, this is not simply the result of living in close proximity, because we know that there are many populated places where a sense of community does not exist. Community depends on connection, and connection determines what we can feel confident depending on one another for.

If your neighbor is merely an acquaintance, you may not feel confident asking him for a stick of butter. Yet, if you know each other well, a stick of butter may be a small thing to ask for. You might even be able to ask him for marriage advice or for help babysitting your kids. The fact that he's your neighbor has nothing to do with it. Your level of connection has everything to do with it.

#6. Connection can prevent desperation.

When you look at what causes us to become disconnected in life, you realize that it's rarely something we knowingly try to do. It happens automatically. Without any outside help, we simply drift into isolation and grow out of touch with people. That is, unless we are continually making efforts to stay connected with them.

If we do this, we are actually meeting some of our basic human needs as well. Because, connection is what lets us feel loved. It's what gives us a sense of belonging and companionship. When we go too long without these needs being met, we aren't the best versions of ourselves. We become lonely, desperate, and needy. Even more, our neediness can begin to drive people away right when we are most hurting for connection with them.

By making it a priority not to get too disconnected from others in the first place, we can altogether avoid getting caught in these lonely cycles of desperation, which can be incredibly hard to get out of.

#7. Connection activates our protective instincts.

Here is another great reason to have strong connections with people; it creates something between you and another person that you both mutually want to protect, contrary to having bad relationships with them and the mutual feeling that there is nothing worth protecting.

People treat things according to how they regard them. They throw garbage away, but they protect and nurture things that they value. So, by improving the quality of your relationship with a person, an amazing transition occurs – you actually advance your relationship with him into a higher place of value in his eyes — one that he regards well and is willing to fight for and preserve.

In short, the easiest way to get good treatment out of people is to have a positive relationship with them. If you do, you automatically inspire them to be kinder, more generous, and more agreeable with you, simply to protect the positive bond they already have with you.

#8. Connection opens the door to trust and credibility.

When you know someone, you know whether or not they are good for what they promise. It may not guarantee that trust will develop; it just creates the possibility for trust to exist. Without connection, relationships cannot really offer you those deep things you desire, like security and expectation. Disconnected relationships seem to stay trapped in the shallow water.

So, now that we've discussed what connecting is, our motives for doing it, and all the benefits that can come out of it, we are ready to talk about what normally stands inbetween us and those benefits. Are you ready? Let's take our conversation to:

CHAPTER 4

BARRIERS

Do you remember the game, "Connect the dots?" It was a simple game that clearly illustrated the concept of connecting. And yet, that same simple concept somehow becomes difficult when we try to apply it to real people. Somehow, when we try to draw lines between ourselves and those other dots around us, our proverbial pens bump into some invisible barriers.

Whether we are aware of these barriers or not, they are there, hindering us. Here is a list of ten of the most common barriers. As you read through this list, please try to see if you recognize any of these barriers affecting you.

Barrier #1. Life changes.

As we age, it is as though we cross a conceptual line somewhere on our paths, and our relationships suddenly become difficult to manage. Our energy levels decrease. We lose motivation. Our responsibilities demand more of our attention. Now, with kids to feed, mortgages to pay for, and careers to sustain, it becomes easy to write off our social connections as luxuries we can no longer afford.

Not to mention, a lot of us have become rusty as we've sat on the sidelines. Like underplayed athletes who have missed entire seasons of practice, we've lost both our familiarity with the sport, as well as our endurance to participate in it.

Meanwhile, we've settled into comfortable niches of familiarity that don't involve as much human interaction or provide much social challenge. We've traded real face time for time on our smartphones and digital devices, and now feel more comfortable sitting in front of a computer screen than we do with actual people.

Barrier #2. False Familiarity.

This is another mental barrier, in which we assume that we are closer to somebody than we actually are. It may be because we have maintained the appearance of being close, such as remaining friends on Facebook, or some other form of social media.

It may be because we share a history with someone, we live close to them geographically, or we're related to them biologically. None of these factors, however, say anything about how connected we actually are to them, or whether or not we know what's going on in their lives.

False familiarity can also come from rumors about a person. If a person has a strong enough reputation, you may feel like you already know him/her before you actually do. This makes false familiarity a difficult barrier for us to see. Few things can keep you from getting to know someone like the belief that you already do.

Barrier #3. Waiting.

This barrier is the one that keeps many of us believing that better opportunities exist somewhere other than in the present moment. There are many different types of waiting. They include:

A. Waiting for others to initiate: This is when a person is convinced that someone else must give him the "green light" before he can go. He almost seems to perceive others as the authority figures in his relationships, and relies on their approval to move forward. In the meantime, he sits alone feeling sad, not realizing that he has a phone – just like everybody else, just as capable of making outgoing calls.

B. Waiting for an excuse. In this case, a person believes that he must always have an excuse to connect, such as groundbreaking news to share or a relevant question to ask. He calls only when he has such a reason, and believes that without one, he can't pick up the phone.

C. Waiting for inspiration. In this case, a person thinks that he should save connecting only for times when he feels like doing it. He assumes that it would be insincere any other time, and because of this, he tends to miss out on precious opportunities.

D. Waiting for the perfect moment. In this case, a person puts off connecting because he believes that there some perfect moment down the road that is ideal for connecting. What he fails to see is that perfect moments rarely ever come. People like this usually have great intentions. They want to give justice to the occasion, and do not want to cheapen it. Yet, they often postpone their efforts indefinitely, despite any great motives they have.

E.Waiting for it to be easy. This is when we fall for the illusion that less energy will be required at a later date. Of course, this isn't true. In fact, something of the opposite is more often true – that the work we put off only becomes more difficult in time.

Now, we should talk about the barrier that is commonly caused by waiting. It is:

Barrier #4. Guilt.

One thing that keeps us from connecting with people is a feeling of guilt for having not been good connectors in the past. A good example of this is when you're at the store, and you see your friend from church, Bob, walking toward you.

You like Bob, and part of you is inclined to say hello. However, another part of you feels guilty for not responding to his last three texts. Oops. You feel bad about it, especially since Bob has been such a nice guy, and has even gone out of his way for you multiple times.

So, as he approaches you, you do what any nice person would do – you pick up a tabloid newspaper and hide your face behind it. He doesn't see you, and walks right on by. "That was close," you think, as a moment of relief comes and goes, quickly followed by the thoughts, "Wow, what's wrong with me? Why did I do that? Bob is a nice guy, and I'm such a jerk."

Guilt is a powerful force. While it can have some rare positive effects in drawing us closer to somebody, it usually works as a wedge, driving us apart from them. Guilt blinds us to opportunities, keeping us focused instead on all the ways that we've failed or fallen short of our intentions. Guilt is why, when you see Bob, you don't really see Bob. You see your own failed efforts to be the kind of person you think you should be to Bob.

Maybe guilt keeps you from seeing your spouse and your children too. Rather than seeing them, you see a lifetime of mistakes or things you wish you had done differently. You see regret and disappointment in yourself, and the feelings that it's too late to start trying.

The end result of guilt is that someone else usually gets punished for our mistakes. Bob gets the brunt of you feeling like a bad friend. Your wife and kids get the brunt of you feeling like a bad husband and father. Is this fair? Not at all.

Also, we should realize that a lot of the guilt we feel is unwarranted and exaggerated, and it can cloud our objectiveness to what is actually true. Bob may not see you at all as you see yourself. He may be a lot more forgiving and understanding toward you than you give him credit for. In truth, your own perfectionism may be what's driving your guilt, causing you to be more critical of yourself than anyone would ever be to you.

Barrier #5. Shyness.

Another common barrier to connection is shyness. The American Psychological Association defines shyness as "the tendency to feel awkward, worried, or tense during social encounters, especially with unfamiliar people." Shyness often involves a person fearing the negative judgments of others.

It is often confused with introversion, although, they are not the same. There are many introverts who aren't shy, and many extroverts who are. Shyness seems to have more to do with a person's belief that there is something wrong with him, and many people who think they have a connection problem really only have a self-perspective problem.

Barrier #6. Fear and invulnerability.

This barrier also has to do with perspective, whereby a person sees the social world as a dangerous arena full of potential threats, such as failure, rejection, and disappointment. He fears the negative consequences of connecting, and therefore, chooses not to engage in it.

Fear can even cause us to be invulnerable, and to hide our true selves from others. If we fear the disapproval of others, we may choose not to let them see who we truly are, attempting to eliminate the possibility of being rejected by them.

Barrier #7. Indirectness.

Because connection can feel so risky, many of us have formed indirect ways of getting what we want. Rather than say what we mean, we hint at it. Rather than let people know we would like to be close to them, we act cool and tough, hoping they will be drawn toward us. It's similar to what animals do in nature, where they puff out their chests and exaggerate their size — simply to attract a mate.

Life has taught us that the prize doesn't always go to the biggest, strongest, or the most direct. Instead, it goes to the most cunning, the most persistent, and the most resourceful - the competitor who calculates and executes his strategy most competently.

Many of us now no longer even know how to be direct with people. For so long, connection has just been a game — one that we have been trying to win at.

Barrier #8. Unresolved personal issues.

This is a big barrier for many of us. One of the main reasons people don't know us is because we don't yet know ourselves. We are in denial about parts of ourselves which we don't want to see or believe in.

This problem often coincides with other problems, such as addictions to alcohol or other substances, which keep a person from clearly seeing reality in the present moment. This is why many people who have gone through painful experiences, such as divorce, the death of a loved one, or abandonment, find it hard to relate with others on their road to recovery.

They are so focused on their own pain and sorrow that they have no energy or attention for anyone else. Some of these people withdraw because they fear being a burden to somebody else. The main point here is that our outward relationships tend to reflect our inner relationship – the one we have with ourselves.

Relationships are fragile, and usually depend on both people maintaining a certain level of health. If a person is prone to jealousy, defensiveness, isolation, snappiness, temper tantrums, or being too easily hurt, she will eventually drive a healthy person away.

Barrier #9. Bad social habits.

This barrier encompasses a large number of undesirable traits and patterns, and can include things like poor hygiene, poor-listening skills, judgmentalness, narcissism, or too much focus on oneself. All of these bad habits tend to make others less interested in connecting with us.

Usually, such things stem from a lack of self-awareness, in which a person does not see himself objectively. He doesn't notice that he continually interrupts people to talk about his cat, or that he checks his texts thirty times during a meal, or that his choice not to wear deodorant is a strong repellant to anyone within ten feet of him.

A lot of us haven't yet come to the realization that we're really rude or smelly or bad at listening, or whatever the case may be. To find out which bad social habits you may have, ask someone in your life who you trust, and who loves you enough to be brutally honest with you. The point here isn't to fish for compliments, but to actually seek criticism that can benefit us overall.

Barrier #10. Autopilot.

This is a mental barrier, in which a person expects the process of connecting to be automatic. And, since he thinks it doesn't require any work, he fails to give it any. Often, this takes place once the hype of a new relationship wears off, and consequently, so does a person's motivation to maintain it.

Relationships suffer or fail when we stop making efforts to sustain them, because, relationships generally tend to require a fair amount of attention and energy. To get our relationships back on track, we must turn off autopilot and regain control.

Barrier #11. Misconceptions.

There are many misconceptions that can affect our ability to connect. For example, we can assume others are just like us when they're not. We can assume they are nothing like us when they are. We can assume that we ourselves are too unlucky or unworthy to connect with them. Or, we can assume that we are fine without them and that we don't really need good connections.

We can assume that connection happens automatically when it really requires effort. We can assume that the future works better for connecting than the present. We can assume that relationships should always be fun, never undergoing moments of conflict or disagreement.

We can assume that we are to blame for our bad connections when the fault may be someone else's. We can assume someone else is to blame when the fault may be our own. We can assume we're doing things wrong when we're doing them right, and vice versa.

We can have misconceptions about what relationships need, what we have to offer them, and what we can hope to get out of them. It is this endless list of misconceptions we can have that stands between us and better connections.

Barrier #12. Opposing desires.

This barrier has to do with anything we desire that directly conflicts with our desires for connection. In other words, it's not that we don't want good connections, it's that we want other things even more.

Yes, you want to have a best friend who shares your interests and goals, but you also want to sit alone and watch TV most evenings. Yes, you want to be friends with your coworkers, but you also want to avoid the possibility of rejection.

Yes, you want to spend quality time with your wife, but you also want to argue with her about why you think you should buy a motorcycle. In most of these cases, you can't have both of the things you desire because they are directly conflicting. Your more dominant desire ends up overpowering any other desire you may have, such as your desire for connection.

Barrier #13. Trying too hard.

We've mentioned that it's common for people to give too little time, energy, and effort. But, is it possible to give too much of these things? The answer is: yes.

We can actually hinder our relationships by going overboard, trying too hard to be funny or fit in or gain the acceptance of other people. We can make ourselves too available and come across as needy. We can ignore subtle cues that others are sending and come across as obnoxious.

As we've said, connection is more of an artform than a science. It is about learning a relationship's fragile balance and giving it what it needs.

SECTION SUMMARY -

So, you have now begun to think about your answers to these four questions:

1. What do you want?

2. Who does it involve?

3. Why do you want it?

4. What stands in your way?

Perhaps you've been wondering where all this is going. All along, we have actually been narrowing down a specific game plan for you. Because, if you are able to identify what normally stops you from reaching your goals, you are one step closer to narrowing down an effective course of action. Slowly but surely, this thought process is aiding you as you work to become a better connector!

Now though, let's talk about some specific concepts and actions that we can focus on to be better connectors.

CHAPTER 5

WAYS TO CONNECT

Previously, we spent a little time talking about how many of us feel too inadequate, too unlucky, or too unworthy to be good connectors. Now, we will address the major problem caused by these beliefs – not just the fact that they hurt us; but the fact that they keep us from seeing the real source of the problem – our technique.

Because, while our thoughts and feelings are important, their importance usually pales in comparison to our actions. Ultimately, our success in life depends on what we do in spite of how we are feeling. As connectors, it is our actions that determine our fates.

Up till now, we've talked about how connecting is not a precise recipe that we can follow from a cookbook. But, this doesn't mean that we should ignore the common general principles of connecting. Because, there definitely are things we can learn to do (or do better) that are sure to improve our connection attempts. Here are some of them.

One of the most simple, powerful things we can do, is:

RECOGNIZE OUR OWN CONTRIBUTION -

As we know, many of our alleged "connection problems" are really just self-perspective problems. We simply aren't sure of what we have to offer. These negative beliefs often keep us from even trying to connect with people. So, it would do us well to learn how to recognize our own contributions. Because, mastering this technique will get us started off on the right foot.

While our self-doubt often hinges upon the fact that we feel we don't have enough trophies on our wall, or the fact that we haven't accomplished enough impressive goals in our lifetimes, the truth is that these things have nothing to do with our importance. Our true importance is our intrinsic value as humans, our relatable experiences, and our ability to empathize and recognize the value in other people. Sometimes, our mere presence alone can mean the world to a person.

If you don't believe me, then look once again at those people you've been most influenced by. Remember that what set them apart wasn't their money, their accolades, or their qualifications. They were normal people who simply gave their presence and time. Aren't you glad that they didn't doubt their contributions? Thankfully, they believed they had something valuable to offer. The moral here is; so should you.

Are you a mother of four who has never seen the world? Don't worry. There are thousands of pregnant women across the country who would love to hear about how you survived – not just physically, but emotionally and financially.

Do you feel like a washed-up middle-aged has-been? Don't worry, there are plenty of young adults who would just like to know how you made it through the doubtful, insecure high-school years. There are people who feel stuck, and who wonder if there is any light for them at the end of their current tunnels. Your wisdom could be worth more to them than gold.

Even if you feel you have no story to share, that's okay too. To add meaning and value to people's' lives, all you need is to be present and available. No qualification is needed to help an elderly woman across the street. No degree is necessary to brighten someone's day with a smile. Without any diploma or credentials, you can still listen to someone who has something heavy to share.

You can hold a baby, give a hug, write a letter of encouragement to a friend, validate someone who feels like a failure, make somebody's telephone ring, say happy birthday, or show up to your nephew's game to cheer him on – all without any special qualifications. When we think too much about whether or not we are qualified, we begin to lose sight of our greatest contribution – who we are. We get caught up thinking about ourselves, rather than about those people we are trying to connect with.

Do you struggle to feel that you have a unique contribution to offer? If so, consider the following quotes and statements:

#1: The US Constitution says that "all men are created equal." In case you weren't sure, this includes you.

#2: Eleanor Roosevelt once said, "Remember always that you not only have the right to be an individual, you have an obligation to be one."

#3: Fred Rogers said that "If only you could sense how important you are to the lives of those you meet; how important you can be to people you may never even dream of. There is something of yourself that you leave at every meeting with another person."

#4: Brigham Young has told us, "Why should we worry about what others think of us, do we have more confidence in their opinions than we do our own?"

#5: Emerson said, "Whatever course you decide upon, there is always someone to tell you that you are wrong. There are always difficulties arising which tempt you to believe that your critics are right. To map out a course of action and follow it to an end requires courage."

RECOGNIZING WHERE YOUR CONTRIBUTION FITS -

Now, it's one thing to recognize your contribution; another thing to know where it best fits. A karate teacher can offer huge contributions in a karate class, but he may not be as versed to contribute at a tea party. There, he would still have a contribution to offer, but he may have to be more creative about his approach. Similarly, each of us should think about how our contributions can match up with other people's needs.

It may help to look at people's various needs, wants, and interests. This will be a good starting point. Perhaps they are looking for a playmate or a companion — someone to do things with or accomplish goals with. Or, someone to laugh with or cry with — a person who will connect with them on an intellectual level. Or, they may want someone that they work well alongside.

They may want a sense of belonging - to feel like they are part of a clan. They may want to be associated with someone who they find cool or attractive. They may want someone to talk to every day. Or, they may only want someone to talk to once in a while.

They may want someone that they look up to as a mentor – someone that they can be a blank canvas to and become molded and shaped by. Or, they may want a mentee – someone they can impart their own wisdom and knowledge to.

How can your contribution(s) meet their specific needs and desires? Or, in other words, how can your contribution be an answer to their specific "why" questions? If you give this some thought, you will probably find ways to add value to people's lives.

SHOWING UP -

As we see, there are no limits to the different ways we can contribute. Nor, to the effects our contributions can have in the lives of those around us. However, there is one thing that most of our contributions have in common; they all require that we "show up."

Woody Allen once said that "Showing up is 80% of life." It's a simple thing, but how often do we fail to see the magnitude of it? It seems that many of us, if anything, have a long list of excuses for why we can't show up.

Showing up is about being present, but more than just physically. It is also about being present mentally and emotionally. It does no good if we show up only to zone out and stare down at our cell phone screens, ignoring what's going on around us. It means bringing our contribution with us – not using it as a chair to rest on.

As a kid, my parents used to come to all of my jazz band concerts. They would actively watch me and cheer me on. They never could afford to buy me a new Mercedes, or to send me away to an expensive ivy league school. But, I feel so blessed and loved by the great gift they did give me – the simple fact that, whenever possible, they wanted to be a part of my life. No other thing could have equated to as much.

Have you ever had somebody show you their love and support by showing up in your life? How did it make you feel? How might you be able to make somebody else feel the same by doing this for them?

LENDING A HELPING HAND -

A few months ago, my friend Matt called and asked me if I could help him with one of his house projects. I asked my wife if she could spare me leaving for a while and she was more than happy to let me go be of assistance.

That afternoon, Matt and I worked hard together in the yard, laughing and talking and catching up in each other's lives. The funny thing is that he and I had been trying to get together for a long time but had both been too busy. Now, who would have guessed that we would be using our busyness to our advantage?

There were a number of ways in which this benefited me. For one, it gave me respect in my wife's eye's, who got to see my helpfulness in action. Also, it gave me respect in my friend's eyes, who was reassured of my loyalty for him. Moreover, it gave me respect in my own eyes. It made me feel good about myself. Best of all though, I got to hang out with a good buddy for a nice portion of time.

Since then, I have learned to see it as an opportunity whenever a friend asks for help. If you're looking to connect with people, look for ways to meet their needs. Are you good with taxes? Help your buddy out who doesn't quite understand them. Are you good with cars? Change that air filter for your cousin who has never done it himself. Small things like this go a long way in building a sense of friendship.

ASKING FOR A HELPING HAND -

Now, I admit, this may seem like a counterintuitive approach to strengthening connections, but please be open-minded. I've actually realized that few things work better to strengthen a bond than when we ask somebody else for help. In fact, this may be even more effective than giving our help to others.

Why? Consider that many people don't like to be on the receiving end of help. They would far rather be givers than takers. They may even feel a sense of shame when they allow themselves to inconvenience anyone else. And yet, these are the same people who would gladly inconvenience themselves to help another person in need. So, if we ask for their help, we are likely to get it.

This is partially because most people look for personal justification for anything that they give their time to. They have an easy time saying no to recreational events, but they have a hard time saying no to a friend in need.

When you ask your friend for help, you aren't inviting him to a barbecue. You're calling on his built-in instinct to assist his fellow man, which is a hard impulse for him to deny. In so doing, you receive the help you need, and he receives an opportunity to do something altruistic. You actually help him meet one of his needs by letting him meet one of yours. Isn't this a good transaction?

Of course, this strategy could easily be abused, so we want to be sure that we never take others' kindness and generosity for granted. However, we also don't want to underutilize their generosity and kindness — choosing never to call on them or accept their assistance in any way. That would be just as erroneous. And, believe it or not, it is the far more common mistake that we make.

SAYING SOMETHING POSITIVE -

While going through paramedic school, I remember being evaluated during our final practical exams. A proctor would sit over our shoulders with a pen and clipboard, judging our abilities to handle the random medical scenarios we were given. In a single do-or-die moment, all we had been taught from class was put to the test. It was extremely nerve-wrecking.

When it was all said and done, we were each given our scores. And, an explanation for why we received the grades we had been given. Not surprisingly, those who did poorly received harsh criticisms. They were told about all they forgot to do or could have done better.

But, when it came time for the higher scorers to receive feedback, I was surprised to find that they too were criticized harshly. In the end, it made no difference whether a person passed or failed. Either way, the only feedback anyone received was negative.

It all showed me something disturbing about the amount of recognition that the average person gets. Most people, despite how well they do, only ever hear about the negative. This helped me see why so many people today feel undervalued. Our hard work behind the scenes rarely ever gets the spotlight. Few of us are regarded for the nine out of ten times we remember to walk the dog, wash the dishes, and bring in the mail. We are regarded for the one time out of ten when we forgot, didn't do it right, or didn't do it quickly enough.

Maybe, this all points to a golden opportunity for us to break into people's worlds. Because, just by giving people this simple affirmation (which they so rarely receive), we can offer them something vital — something that they are starving for.

Can you find something good to mention about your spouse? Your brother? Your best friend? You may not think there is anything good to say about these people. If so, this actually implies more about you than them. It means you've grown accustomed to seeing only the negative in some, and that you are a top candidate for a perspective readjustment.

Giving good feedback is easy and it costs nothing. It may actually be the simplest and surest way to brighten up another person's life. You just have to be looking and you just have to be verbal. That's it.

RECIPROCATING -

Have you ever told a joke to somebody who didn't laugh or smile? Have you ever sent a text message to a friend who never bothered to respond? These are a few examples of poor reciprocation.

The word "Reciprocation," by definition, means: "A mutual exchange." When you make any kind of effort to connect with somebody, your hope is that they will respond in a similar way to you.

When you do something kind or considerate for a person, she may reciprocate by saying "Thank you." When a friend calls and leaves you a message, you reciprocate by returning his call. If you don't do your part in the exchange, you are damaging your relationships.

John Gottman, relationships expert and author of many books, including The Relationship Cure, refers to these efforts for connection as "bids." When somebody makes a bid at you, they are hoping that you will bid back. If you repeatedly fail to do this, a person will usually stop bidding, sensing that a desire for connection is not mutual.

CONNECTING WITH PEOPLE IN THEIR TIMING -

The truth is, people aren't always bidding our way. Sometimes they are too busy. Sometimes they have other plans or interests. Occasionally though, their interests are focused directly on us and it becomes crystal clear that they want our attention.

These are the moments when we don't have to wonder if they are interested – they've already shown us! In fact, these may be the only occasions on earth when there is no guesswork involved in the timing of connection.

When your friend texts you and asks how you're doing, your co-worker emails you with a question, or your nephew asks you if you can take him fishing, you are presented with some significant opportunities.

We often don't see the significance of these opportunities simply because they seem so small. We think, "It's just a text. Just an email. Just a request for my time." So, since these opportunities don't jump out at us as powerful ways to make relationships strong, we miss them.

But, connection, when you break it down, is kind of like a snowball – not just a single mass, but a collection of many tiny snowflakes. Every single interaction with a person works together with the others to form something big – a relationship.

A joke is met with laughter. A friendly glance is met by a friendly glance. Little by little, the door to familiarity opens and new chances for interaction become possible. The relationship grows.

But, if we constantly ignore these small chances to connect, our proverbial snowballs stop growing. Worse yet, they start to melt. Little by little, we grow distant in our relationships. Usually, in such small ways that we don't even notice until a significant puddle has formed.

So, in order to keep our proverbial snowballs from melting, we must learn to connect with people on their time – when it is most convenient for them. Because, every bid has a lifespan. If we wait too long to act, our opportunities will melt before our eyes.

To cash in on these opportunities, we must simply learn to make time. In other words, give up a half hour of your busy day to take your nephew fishing. Take thirty seconds to respond to that text, even if you'd rather do it later. And even if you don't have a perfect response to that coworker's email, just say, "Thanks. I'll get back to you soon." Even a small and imperfect response is better than none at all.

Most people simply won't wait around until we feel ready. If we ignore our friends bids, they'll find somebody else to talk to who gets back to them sooner. Your nephew will eventually lose interest in fishing with you. Or, he'll figure out how to do it on his own. Heck, he may even be fishing with nephews of his own by the time you finally feel ready.

Taking action now will help you seize important moments before they are gone. And, it will free up your mind, giving you one less thing to feel guilty about.

That small amount of time you take to respond, you'll find, is usually only slightly inconvenient, but not impossible. And, you'll probably also find that you have simply formed a habit of saying no – not because you can't say yes now, but because no is always easier.

Even though we usually have great reasons for putting things off, who cares? If our relationships end up suffering, does it matter how great our excuses are? Life rarely goes as we plan anyway. Some of the best moments are the ones that happen spontaneously and the ones that we plan often fall short of our expectations. So, let's quit postponing our actions for a perfect moment that will probably never come.

Let's learn that when people make efforts to reach out to us, these are golden, once-in-a-lifetime opportunities that might never come again. When people bid our way, they are doing the work of connecting for us. All we have to do is be smart enough (and quick enough) to act on it.

RELATING TO PEOPLE THEIR WAY -

Wouldn't it be great if connection happened on your terms? If all your friends and relatives came to you and took a passion in what you love doing? What if your nephews and nieces just loved talking with you about golf and politics? What if your in-laws just couldn't hear enough of your knowledge about woodwork? That would be amazing, but it's not going to happen.

In real life, we have to learn how to connect with others their way. Breaking into their worlds usually means breaking out of our own comfort zones. It isn't always easy, which is part of why we don't always do it. But, we must learn to do what works for others. Because, what has always worked for us may not be what works for them.

Your nephew isn't just like you. He's quiet and introverted. He might never care about your political opinions, and if you try to engage with him this way, you might never gain ground. But, he might love nothing more than to play you in a game of chess. If you break into his world, you won't have to drag him kicking and screaming into yours.

It is good to forge our way into the lives of others, but this usually involves learning to share their interests. However, when we do, we may feel like we are being insincere. After all, if you think chess is boring, you may feel like your attempt to show interest in it isn't genuine. But, try to think of it as work. Because, you don't have to like something in order to give it your effort. You just have to have a reason to try.

Once you begin doing this work, you may even discover your own interests expanding. As your knowledge of chess grows, you may no longer feel like you are pretending to like it. Sincerity can come over time. That is, if you are determined to teach yourself to care about what others are interested in.

LOOKING FOR COMMON GROUND -

Sometimes, in order to break into other people's worlds, we don't even have to leave our own. If we're looking, we can find places where our worlds overlap. This is the easiest way to unite with other people.

You have something in common with everyone. Even if you were to find somebody on this earth who was your complete opposite in some areas, you would still find things that you have in common in other areas.

To start, let's look at the basics. You both drink water and you both breathe air. You both eat food and you both are held down by gravity. You both depend on shelter and you both need connection. Are we doing okay so far? Good! Let's see if we can keep going!

Maybe you've both visited some of the same places. Maybe you both traverse the same highway on your way to work. Maybe you share mutual friends. The point is to open your mind to what you might have in common, or you risk getting stuck only seeing what you don't.

We humans are often much better at noticing differences than similarities. Before we have even begun to see how much a person is like us, we've already taken notice of all the ways that he isn't. We notice differences in skin color, fashion, speech, and age. We get stuck on the ways people differ from us politically and religiously.

But, if we train ourselves to look for areas of common ground instead, we will always be able to find them.

What we notice, in the end, is really only proof of one thing — what we were looking for in the first place. Since we tend to find what we're looking for, let's look for the good. Let's look for similarities, rather than differences.

Try to find at least a few areas of common ground with people you would like to connect with. Once you have found a few, try to keep them in focus in your mind. You may find just how many wonderful qualities there are to discover in people — hidden right beneath the surface of what our eyes notice at first glance.

DOING THINGS TOGETHER -

As I look back at some of the friends I've had in life, I notice a common mystery — the fact that many of my friends were complete opposites to me. In some cases, we were so different that I'm amazed we ever even became friends. And yet, we did. Why? Perhaps, the answer lies somewhere in the fact that we did things together.

Brent and I have very different personalities. And yet, that didn't seem to matter at all when we were out running, canoeing, and bike riding together on those hot summer afternoons.

Todd and I were different too, but neither of us even seemed to notice it while we were playing chess for hours on end. Sometimes we'd talk, but a lot of times, we wouldn't. A lot of times, we'd play video games down in the basement without ever noticing how different we were as people.

Scott and I have always been pretty very different as well, but those differences seemed to vanish when we were out walking on the railroad tracks, shooting at cans with our slingshots, just as my good friend Matt and I would forget how different we were when we were out climbing those steep rocks together up at Devil's Lake State Park.

It's funny how we never worried about creating dialogue in these moments. We never sat down Indian style to face each other with the intent of having a heart-to-heart. We were just doing an activity that we both enjoyed. And yet, these activities united us more than anything else could.

I've come to see that most great connections happen when connection isn't even our aim. And that, whenever we are wrapped in a common task with somebody, our differences somehow seem to vanish. In fact, it almost becomes impossible not to form a connection with them.

If you want to connect with somebody, it may be as simple as finding just one thing that you can do together. A jigsaw puzzle. A card game. A walk through the park or a bike ride. If you find something you can do together, connection will most likely be the result that happens in an almost effortless way.

TALKING -

While there are ways of connecting that don't require talking, sometimes, talking is inevitable. At work, in the church lobby, and in other social gatherings, we find our ability to gab being called upon and challenged. How can we become good conversationalists when we need to be?

Starting a conversation can be hard. Because of this, it may do us well to look at people who are great at handling conversations. They are the masters. There must be something we can learn by observing them.

For starters, it's easy to see that they are usually exceptional listeners. They have a way of making you feel at ease. They give reassuring looks and gestures and ask relevant questions, inviting you to share and open up. So, these must be some of the traits we can learn to exhibit.

Bad conversationalists, on the other hand, tend to sit there like a bump on a log, offering blank stares and one-word answers. They leave the entire weight of the conversation for you to carry. These must be some of the traits we can learn to check at the door.

When you approach somebody to begin a conversation, you may start with a greeting or a comment about last night's game. This initial phase of a conversation could be called the "interview" phase. Because, both people are still feeling each other out, trying to find a common direction for the conversation to go in.

They are watching each other closely for subtle signs, determining if the other is really interested and if there is any reason to keep the conversation going. At this point, it could easily lose momentum if one or both people aren't reciprocating well.

If one person fails to acknowledge what the other has said, or if one person keeps looking down at his phone as though to check the time, it will most likely communicate disinterest, bringing the conversation to a rapid end.

We can also indirectly end conversations by giving replies that are too long, too short, too irrelevant, or too closed-ended. Here, it is especially important that we are sensitive to others when they are talking – that we show interest, be good listeners, give relevant responses, and be inquisitive.

Here, reciprocation is key. If somebody comments on the score of last night's big game, it will help to do more than simply nod and agree. Better yet, try giving the conversation a direction to go in.

Open-ended questions can be very useful. These are questions that require more than a yes or no answer. You could respond to that comment about the game with, "Who were you going for?" or, "What is your favorite sport?"

This can be helpful because: A, it leads to more in depth interactions, and: B, it gives the person a chance to talk about his own thoughts and feelings. One other added bonus to this approach is that it keeps you out of the spotlight – a place that many of us don't like to be.

Body language too can either help or hurt. This includes all the nonverbal things that you do, whether consciously or subconsciously, such as folding your arms, slouching, leaning back, or yawning. Your body is always saying something – even when your lips are not. So, be sure not to send indirect messages that confuse the person you're talking to.

Some helpful body language might include:

- Making eye-contact.

- Nodding your head to show that you are engaged.

- A welcoming posture, such as leaning forward or positioning yourself so that you are facing the speaker.

- Facial expressions that convey a proper emotional response to what is being said.

Once the interview phase has ended, the conversation will either end or go deeper into more specific subjects. If you get past the interview, this is a good thing. It means you have succeeded in finding a common ground with somebody, and your conversation can live on long enough to discover even more common grounds.

LISTENING -

Listening is an important aspect of communicating with anyone. But, in many marriages, friendships, family relationships, and even in many work relationships, people feel that their words fall on deaf ears. And, it's easy to see why; many of us are terrible listeners.

We don't try to give our full attention to those around us, we are constantly hypnotized and distracted by our phones, we aren't really interested in what we could learn from people, or we just haven't made it a priority to be attentive.

There are many reasons why we might fail as listeners. It may be because we are too busy assuming we already know what a person is saying. While we watch their lips moving, our minds are elsewhere — coming up with a good argument or thinking about the game.

Or, it could be because we are uncomfortable with something. Perhaps, silence. We feel awkward whenever there are gaps in a conversation, and we race to fill them in with noise. We may even do this with good intent, thinking that we are lightening the mood for somebody else. But, we're not. We're just hindering dialog and robbing someone else of his/her chance to feel heard.

Other times, we aren't good listeners because we are uncomfortable with the subject matter at hand. We are scared off by the mention of politics, religion, death, deep emotions, or controversial subjects.

The funny thing is, we usually avoid these subjects because we are convinced that other people are uneasy with them, and we feel like we are doing them a service by avoiding them. But, what if those tough subjects are what somebody else wants to talk about? If they aren't uncomfortable, why should we be?

In order to be a good listener, you don't have to like what is being talked about. You don't have to love or agree with every comment made. You just have to hear it and acknowledge it. Acknowledging somebody's point of view doesn't mean that you are adopting it yourself.

We may also be bad listeners because we are overbearing. As soon as it's our turn to talk, we spout out all we can about all of our own thoughts and feelings. When we do this, we aren't having a conversation; we are dominating one.

Those of us who dominate conversations are usually unaware that we do it.   If ever we could see our conversations written out on paper, we would be embarrassed by the amount of space taken up by our words, compared to the small amount of space we've given to others.

Since good listening is so rare, it is actually one of the greatest gifts we can give. And, it is an easy gift to give, being that most people have something to share. Your cousin is excited to talk about his new job. Your uncle is proud of the shed he built in the back. Your sister is frustrated by her best friend's new boyfriend. In all of these cases you can make large strides toward connection simply by being a good listener.

While you may not be able to fix each person's problems, you can shoulder an enormous burden for them just by allowing them to get something off their chests, which will win you large connection points with them. Especially when you listen well!

FIGURING OUT WHAT WORKS FOR YOU -

It seems that we hear a lot of advice these days, but, is all of that advice good? It may not always apply to us as individuals, because we are each unique. While some generalities may contain some universal truth, many of them leave no room for exceptions, which, there are plenty of in this world — myself, included.

For example, I have a few quirks of my own that have always made listening into a challenge for me. One is: I feel pressured to assure people that I am following along — so much that it sometimes actually distracts me from listening. I can actually become so concerned about appearing focused that it actually causes me to lose my focus. Even though I'm nodding and smiling and making eye contact, people's messages are going in one ear and out the other.

So, I have learned that I must reevaluate what I know about listening and try to find strategies that work for me. Because, it doesn't matter if I'm listening the way everyone thinks I should. It matters that I'm doing it in a way what actually works.

If you're anything like me, you too may feel that conventional advice doesn't always work for you. And, you too may have to come up with your own techniques in order to be a good listener.

At times, when I've been distracted, I've actually chosen not to make eye-contact. I've found that it was too distracting, and that I was actually much better at listening when I wasn't being distracted by a person's movements, looks, and gestures.

Once or twice, I have even found it helpful to imagine a person's words being typed out on paper as he speaks, allowing me to visualize his words, rather than simply hear them. I know. It's strange, but it's one of those tricks that has actually helped me.

Again, these practices aren't conventional. Nor are they necessarily what I would even recommend. I'm simply telling you to be creative and figure out what works for you. You are your own unique person and there is no one-size-fits all bit of advice.

GENERAL TIPS FOR BEING A GOOD LISTENER -

In regards to actual steps we can take to be good listeners, I've found that there are a few general rules that we should all try to keep. They are:

Keep your phone out of view.

These days, phones are everywhere. People are always texting and talking wherever they go – in grocery lines, on buses, and in waiting rooms. And, a large number of people are offended by the way these devices intrude on their own chances at personal interaction. So, it would be good for us to put our phones away when we are with people that we are trying to give our attention to.

Not only is this good for them, it's good for us. Most of us are too easily distracted to be effective multi-taskers. If we simply turn off the sound on our phones and place them into our pockets, they are much less likely to distract us and offend others.

Avoid distracting backgrounds.

While it's great that you've turned your phone off, it doesn't help that you've chosen to sit at the bar top table that has a large screen TV right above your wife's head. Chances are, you're not going to have a real heart-to-heart in this situation – especially if the Packers start to lose and you don't like the calls that the ref is making.

When you know you are going to be with somebody and your attention will be required, try to set yourself up for success by choosing a position that has the fewest distractions. This will automatically lighten the burden that listening may be for you.

Be present and be intentional.

When it comes to being a good listener, be intentional about listening. If you lose focus, bring it back. Redirect your attention as often as it gets lost. Stay in the room with the person you are in the room with, because it's so easy to let our minds wander elsewhere and miss out on beautiful opportunities to connect.

HUMOR -

Humor is another one of those things that can help a conversation along. It can bring energy to it. It can break down walls of tension. It can unite us and brighten our worlds. It can give us a sense of closeness and make us smile and laugh, which is, as they say, the best medicine.

When we engage in genuine laughter with another person, we are breaking free of our own rigid thought patterns and doing something spontaneous. We are allowing our own perspectives to be broadened. Often, this opens the door to creativity and problem solving that might otherwise stay barred shut.

When two friends share an inside joke, it is like they share a special language that only they understand. No one else gets it, which is part of what makes it funny. It can happen by a single word or look. Instantly, both people are reminded of a memory. They each feel a unique sense of closeness and are drawn together.

However, despite the many great ways that humor can be used for good, it is something that must be used discerningly. While a well-told joke can lighten moods and bring people together, a poorly told joke can make people uneasy. An off-color joke can be offensive.

Humor has a way of being lost in translation. The jokes you tell your fishing buddies probably won't work for aunt Bertha. And, the jokes that work for kids probably won't work for adults, who, quite frankly, may not care about why the chicken crossed the road. If you insist on telling them, they may cross the road themselves… to get away from you.

With such a vast array of potential outcomes that humor can bring, it may be helpful to look at it more closely.

Maybe we can figure out what separates good uses of humor from bad. Here are a few things to keep in mind.

For starters, humor is supposed to be funny. It's not funny when it is used to cover up certain emotions. When there are facts that need to be faced, feelings that need to be dealt with, or actual threats that need to be addressed, avoidance is anything but funny – even if it is done in a humorous way. We should be careful not to let humor be a mask for unpleasant truths.

Also, if you attempt a joke, don't let someone else be the butt of it. Humor is usually only funny when more than one person is laughing. If your joke implies anything that's mean, insulting, or critical to the other person, you will probably find your attempts failing to create smiles.

Other things to keep in mind when using humor -

Delivery -

As the old saying goes, "Some people know how to tell a joke. Some people don't." We've all had somebody bust a wisecrack, which, for whatever reason, simply was not funny. We may not have even been able to put a finger on why it wasn't funny. Perhaps the joke itself wasn't all that bad, but something about it didn't bring about the desired response. Most likely, it had to do with the way it was delivered.

Good delivery has a lot to do with your own level of confidence, your tone, your body language, and your word choices. And, it has a lot to do with:

Timing -

Some of the best comedians are known for their timing, or, their masterful ability to seize a moment, utilizing quick wit and intuition. They show us that when it comes to being funny, nailing the timing is half the battle.

When you boil it down, timing has to do with contextual relevance. Topics tend to change many times during a conversation, and we only have small windows of opportunity to make relevant comments. Humor isn't just about what you say, it's about when you say it.

In a way, you could almost say that humor is like an itch. Scratching it only feels good if you scratch while it's itching. Any other time, a scratch is just hurtful or annoying. We've all known the discomfort of listening to a speaker who gets his timing wrong. Often, it embarrasses everyone – not just the speaker, but the listeners as well.

If humor is an artform, then timing is like a paintbrush. The painter must know just how to use it in order to create his masterpiece. Those who use it best are the ones have an objective view of themselves and their listeners.

Setting -

As a general rule, a funeral probably isn't the best setting for joke-telling. Nor is church, while the preacher is talking, or traffic court, while the judge is addressing the courtroom. Formal dinners, libraries, and study halls might also be added to this list.

In these settings, humor comes at someone else's expense. While a joke may seem like a good way to lighten up otherwise dull situations, if the setting is wrong, you may only rub somebody the wrong way. And, give them a bad impression of you.

Hopefully, all of this gives you something to chew on as you try to become a decent conversationalist. Whether or not you agree with my thoughts exactly, you should discover what works for you and use it to better yourself at building conversations. In the end, it will only make you more relatable to others and strengthen your bonds with them.

CONNECTING WITH KIDS -

Finally, we should close this section by talking a little bit about connecting specifically with children. If you have or know children that you would like to know better, maybe you've found it challenging to break into their worlds. Maybe you've realized that the normal rules of connecting that apply with adults, don't always apply with kids. What can we say we know about children?

For one, we can say that the small things seem to matter to them. Because, even though we may throw them big parties, buy them expensive presents, and take them to exciting places, the magnitude of our gift tends to get lost on them. Instead, they remember the little things that you and I may not have even noticed.

The little bits of time we gave them our full attention. The moments we made them feel special. The moments we let them know that we were glad just to be with them. You see? No big party is needed to create the most memorable events.

Of course, not all kids are the same, and their interests tend to vary depending on age group. A one-year old may be fascinated by a leaf he found on the ground, whereas a five year old may be interested in learning to ride a bike, and a ten year old may already be into pop music and sports.

We can easily over-generalize children without our knowing, which is actually a large part of why it can be a struggle for us to connect with them. Who likes to be patronized? Who likes to be treated like a clone? Nobody. Especially not children.

This is one area where we can easily try too hard and be off-putting unintentionally, thinking we have to be funny or clever or fancy. Really, we just have to be good listeners. We just have to engage with them and try to be a part of whatever they are a part of.

To do this, try these two things:

#1. Try to see the world through their eyes.

Children see the world differently. Things that are old and boring to us are new and exciting to them. Things like shaving, driving a car, or having no curfew, are part of a world that they only gaze upon as outsiders. We must remember that.

Try to rediscover the wonder that we adults so easily overlook. Try to see their world, not from above looking down, but from beside them, looking out. Allow yourself to be a kid at heart. Let yourself explore your own silly, crazy side. Jump on a couch, if that's what they're doing. You may even get them to forget that you're a few decades older and and a few feet taller.

#2. Look for common ground.

Don't forget that you were once a kid too. Is it that hard to remember? You once took your first steps. You once wanted a little red wagon for Christmas. You once learned how to ride a bike and used it to deliver papers on your paper route. You once had a favorite color, a favorite toy, a favorite sweet cereal, and a favorite park to play at.

Try to see how these things can give you common ground with the kids you are trying to connect with. Your position in life may be much different than theirs, but that doesn't mean you haven't been in their position. Try to see how your own memories and experiences may relate with theirs. It doesn't take much effort. It just takes your own memories. And, a dash of imagination.

CONNECTING ONE-ON-ONE -

I've found that there is power in connecting with people one-on-one. When possible, it may help your situation to single a certain person out and get him/her to migrate away from the party. This way, you may find yourself being a better listener. You'll probably find it easier to give all your energy and focus to a single person, rather than having to split your focus multiple ways.

The one-on-one approach is especially great for kids. And, for anyone who is introverted, or, uncomfortable in group settings. If ever you find it difficult to connect with someone in a group setting, the one-on-one approach could be your secret weapon.

CHAPTER 6

MAKING A CONNECTION JOURNAL

I remember when I heard the sad news that my uncle Rob had passed away. He had been helping somebody fill a moving truck when he collapsed in the driveway and died of a sudden heart attack.

The news stunned me in a sad, surreal way. I couldn't believe it. I had always felt a special tie with my uncle

Rob because he had always been intentional about having a relationship with me.

Throughout my life, he had been there for me during big events. He called me when I graduated and wrote to me when I was getting married. He sent me birthday cards and would occasionally email me to ask me about my life. Even though he lived a thousand miles away, he was one of my closest relatives.

At his funeral, I listened as people shared their sentiments. I was surprised at how many others had the same strong type of connection with him that I had. It became clear to me that Rob was a rare, unique type of connector, and that I was only one of the many lucky people who knew him.

While it was heartbreaking to lose him, I came home from that trip feeling inspired to strengthen my relationships with the people in my life. I realized that anyone can be a good connector. You don't have to be born good at it. You just have to care about others and break into their worlds… the way uncle Rob did.

One day while I was thinking about it all, I got this crazy idea about how I could strengthen my relationships with nearly everyone that I knew. I would call it "My connection journal." Basically, it would be a schedule for staying in touch with all the people that mattered to me.

I sat my computer and began hammering away, making a list of virtually every person I knew – family members, friends, acquaintances, coworkers, and fellow church members – and I began to rate them on a scale from one to five according to how close I was to each of them.

People I had known a long time, such as my brothers and sisters, were given a one. People who I knew well but did not have a strong relationship with, such as certain coworkers and acquaintances in my neighborhood, were given a three. People I barely knew at all and rarely ever saw, such as distant friends in other states and countries, were given a five, and so on.

Under each person's name there was a small journal section where I could write down any notes about each person that I thought were pertinent. Peter loves photography. David traveled to China four times last year. Ron goes to the same church as Aunt Diane, etc. This gave me a starting point for each person I wanted to strengthen my connections with. And, a point of reference for future conversations.

By the time I was done, I had developed a scheduling system for staying in touch with each person according to the rating I had given them. Those people who I had given a 1 ranking, such as my brothers and sisters, I would try to stay in touch with once a week. Those people with a 2 ranking, I might try to stay in touch with every other week, and so on. Those people with a lower ranking, such as those distant friends in other states and countries, I might only reach out to once or twice a year.

I found an app that let me enter all this data into it and it turned that data into reminders that would go off whenever it was time to connect with somebody. For example, I'd receive a message in my tray, saying, "David." If I opened it up, I would see all of the notes I had written about David. I could read about our last discussion or certain events in his life. Then, when it was time to give him a call, I felt like I had a good direction to go in. I wasn't just calling with nothing to say.

Of course, since I originally began creating this system, it has changed quite a bit. One reason for this is the fact that I lost the phone that had all my information stored in it. Not to mention, the app I once used is no longer on the market.

These days, I've discovered that Facebook can pretty much do all the same stuff for me. It notifies me about birthdays and big events of all my friends and family members. And, if I keep in touch with these people on Facebook messenger, it automatically saves our prior conversations, making it incredibly easy to refresh my memory about the last conversations we've had.

Anyway, at the risk of sounding nerdy, I say all this because I believe that having some type of system is beneficial. Perhaps, even needed. I'm the type of person who does very well with reminders, because I'm not naturally structured and am somewhat prone to forgetting.

While you may not want to go to the extent I did, I think it would be wise for you to have some type of system for staying in touch with the people you care about. Let's spend a little time right now talking about why this is beneficial.

THE BENEFITS OF USING A CONNECTION JOURNAL -

The idea of a connection journal has to do with keeping track of the many different aspects of your relationships. It can include documenting the thoughts you have about a person, the inside jokes you share, the things you want to remember to tell that person, or the things you talked about last time you were together.

It can include details about a particular person that you want to remember, such as the type of work that she does, the number of kids she has, how long she's been married, what's important to her, and what her interests and personality type are. It can include her birthday, her anniversary date, or other special dates that she cares about remembering. Each bit of information you use is a key into that can be used to open the door to her world.

CONNECTION CHECKPOINTS -

These days, there are a thousand and one ways to stay in touch with people, whether you use social media, texting, telephone, or video calls. Take your pick. You may find that certain avenues of connecting work better than others with certain people.

For example, texting might be the ideal way to keep in touch with your sister, but it might not work with your Aunt Judy who still uses a flip phone and doesn't even know what a text message is.

Facebook is another great way to stay in touch with people. Now, I don't want to confuse you, because I talked about Facebook earlier in the book as a potential pitfall, which can give us a sense of false familiarity with people. While it is true that Facebook (and other social media like it) can be misused, these things can also be wonderful, practical tools for staying in touch with people. That is, if we know their limitations.

Consider that a good deal of the people you know on Facebook are more than just "Facebook friends," they are your actual friends in real life. You probably have a lot of close family members, relatives, and coworkers on Facebook who use it regularly. Why not utilize this platform as an additional way of interacting with people?

Your cousin in North Dakota just posted that he reached his weight loss goal for the summer. Your sister mentioned something funny that her two-year-old daughter said this morning. Your buddy said that it's his son's birthday. In each of these cases, you can show somebody that you care simply by leaving a comment.

We often fail to see these valuable opportunities to stay current in one another's lives. No, Facebook will not bridge all gaps between you and the people you care about, but it can bridge some of them.

My rule of thumb for social media is this: use it, but don't let it be your only way of staying connected with people. I say, take advantage of every method you can for staying in touch, because there have never been so many fun, convenient options at our fingertips.

YOUR CONNECTION JOURNAL - WHAT IT IS. WHAT IT ISN'T.

If you make a list as I have done and if you decide to rank people similarly, please understand that the way you rank them does not reflect how much you love, respect, or value them. It reflects how much maintenance you think your relationship with them needs.

The fact that your wife ranks lower than your brother is simply because your relationship with your wife is already strong, and your relationship with your brother is not. This is similar to a medical triage system for treating patients. The system does not prioritize people according to their value as humans, but according to the urgency of their needs.

The connection journal is merely a helpful way of remembering to connect with people that we might otherwise forget to stay in touch with. It is about taking charge of all our relationships — not just the ones that are easy and fun for us to maintain, but also, the ones that somehow slip out of sight and out of mind.

But, since many people might not understand this, it may be wise for you to treat your connection journal like you would any other journal, reserving its contents for your eyes only. This decreases your risks of ever hurting your loved ones unnecessarily or having to explain your way out of a jam with them.

LEARNING TO CONNECT THROUGH ROLE MODELS -

My uncle Rob showed me some valuable things about connecting with people. Because I knew him, I got to see a master at work. And, I believe that there may be no better way to learn than by having a skilled person to emulate.

In fact, I believe that we all need role models in our lives – people who we admire in some way who we can learn from. Couldn't you learn a lot by studying certain people and doing what they do? If they're techniques work so well for them, shouldn't they work for you as well?

Many people are turned off by the idea of having a role model because it feels ingenuine. They don't want to adopt techniques and strategies that are not their own. They see it as plagiarizing or as pirating another person's intellectual property. However, this is not true.

As the saying goes, "Imitation is the highest form of flattery." By imitating someone, you are indirectly giving your respects to that person and saying that his strategy is worthy of replication. It doesn't mean you should become a clone of that person. It just means that you want to adopt his techniques in your own original way.

OTHER ROLE MODELS THAT HAVE INSPIRED ME -

Apart from uncle Rob, there have been a few other role models in my life that I have chosen to learn from. In fact, I have different role models for different skill sets. Because, different people are gifted in different areas.

MY NETWORKING ROLE MODEL -

As far as good networkers go, there are few people I know who are as skilled as my friend, Kevin. Kevin and I were in the same rock band together for the better part of 10 years. He joined our band when we were just a group of unorganized musicians, hoping to make it big.

Unlike the rest of us, Kevin was very structured. His primary skills and contributions were more managerial than musical. He was a master at planning, organizing, and networking. He was business-minded and had good follow through, keeping in touch with a whole crowd of people that we met along the way and turning those acquaintances into relationships.

If you called Kevin, he would always call you back. If you texted him, you could expect a timely response. If you were a local camp director emailing him about availability or rates, Kevin would not let your email sit in his inbox, collecting dust. He would get back to you quickly and make sure to answer all of your questions. He was just that good.

But, he was just as good at doing this with his friends and band members. He never let us feel like we weren't a priority. He never made us wonder if he had gotten our voicemails or if our questions would forever go unanswered.

Because of his amazing networking skills, our band was soon playing high-paying gigs every weekend and our audience began to expand across the country. We even played in Japan twice on all-expense-paid trips. I feel confident saying that none of this would have happened if not for him.

Most of all, Kevin helped me see that this was an area that I desperately needed to grow in. He inspired me much the way that Uncle Rob did. Now, I make more of an effort to hold up my end in my communications with other people, which has also made me more confident in my approach with them.

MY EMPATHY ROLE MODEL -

When it comes to being empathetic, few people I know compare to my cousin, Wade. While he is a cousin, he is also a great friend.

Years ago, when we were kids up at summer camp, a group of us went swimming in the lake. While we were there, I stepped on a sharp stone that was submerged under water. A tiny piece of that stone broke off inside my foot. Wade saw that I was in pain and immediately rushed over to my rescue. He stood beside me and helped me hobble on down to the camp infirmary.

When we got there, the nurse took a look at my foot and pulled out a sharp metal utensil from her bag. She wiped my foot with some kind of disinfectant and began trying to remove the stone. Needless to say, I was in a great deal of pain and fearful of the process.

One thing that comforted me was the fact that Wade was beside me. I knew I wasn't alone. But not only that, Wade somehow made me feel like my problem was his own. In fact, he even seemed to be more bothered by my pain than I was.

I know. Toe injuries are small in the grand scheme of all that can go wrong in a human's existence. Yet, I think that's actually what makes me value Wade's concern so much. Even though the injury was minor, it was a big deal to him. He cares when someone is even a little bit afraid. That, to me, is significant.

In small ways like this, Wade has proven himself an exemplary friend many times over the years. And, he has inspired me to be more empathetic to others and to try caring for their problems like they are my own.

MY SOCIAL/CONNECTION ROLE MODEL -

My friend and coworker, Dylan, is a natural at breaking into people's worlds. He's one of those guys that can just make friends with anyone in just minutes. He is friendly, outgoing, and personable. He is accepting and loves making people smile.

Sometimes, when we work together, I like to sit back and watch him interacting with others. I've noticed that he laughs a lot and listens well to what people say. He commonly finds ways to agree with people, saying things like, "That's what I'm talking about," or, "Now you're speaking my language."

Talking to Dylan is just fun, because you find yourself laughing and feeling accepted. He's comfortable in his own skin, which makes you feel comfortable in yours. And, you never run out of things to talk about, because he's a pro at keeping the conversation going.

By hanging around Dylan, I feel that I become a better connector. His optimism and ease rub off on me. They are contagious. I'm glad to have people like him in my life who help make me a more well-rounded connector.

SECTION SUMMARY -

So, these are just a few of the people in my life who I call "role models" in some way, shape, or form. And, as you can see, they each model different types of strengths. Each has different giftings and has taught me where I can become more well-rounded a person, and has given me some direction as to how. I am grateful for their examples in my life, and will always strive to follow their lead.

I only hope that you as well have certain people in your life who you can model after. If so, they are a blessing. If not, I would suggest that you find people you can emulate. Or, change your environment, because we all need people in our lives who we look up to, and who demonstrate for us what we cannot do.

LEARNING TO CONNECT THROUGH MENTORS -

Role models are extremely important. They teach us a lot through demonstration. Mentors, however, do more than simply demonstrate. They interact with us one-on-one. They are people we can share our thoughts with, ask questions to, and request help from in specific matters. In short, mentors are people who help us become role models ourselves.

My uncle was a great role model, but he wasn't my mentor. A lot of what I learned from him was learned from a distance. Much of it, even after he was gone. Because, a role model doesn't even have to be someone that you know. It can be a famous athlete, a historical figure, or an author that you admire.

A mentor, however, is someone you know and who knows you, who has agreed to work with you and coach you in the area where you seek assistance. If we long to be better connectors, it could be especially beneficial for us to seek out a mentor.

Perhaps you've noticed that there is a certain type of magic that transpires when we work closely with someone we want to learn from. We seem to gain some of their essence just by being in their company.

Bob Dylan was mentored by Woodie Guthrie. Oprah Winfrey was mentored by Maya Angelou. Quincy Jones was mentored by Ray Charles, and Mother Theresa was mentored by her father, Michael Van Der Peet.

To be great at anything, it is helpful to have someone great to model after. But, even better, is to have the help of someone who has agreed to be your mentor.

Greatness simply is not easy to replicate. If it was, everyone would be great, and "great" would just be another synonym for "average." Not to mention, many people who are great at something lack the ability to understand and explain what makes them great.

This is why it is helpful to let them guide you and shape you, much the way that a baby cub learns from its mother how to catch prey. Sometimes, explanations aren't needed – just one-on-one interacting until the practiced artform becomes mastered.

If you seek out a mentor to guide you along in the ways of connecting, you'll probably find that some people are glad to impart their skill and knowledge to you – flattered, even, to know that you seek it.

You can give people a sense of pride and joy by asking them to help you in an area where you are weak and they are strong, so don't be timid about asking. If you have a mentor in mind, this may be a great chance for you to grow and learn from her, and even strengthen your connection with her.

Tell her sometime that you admire the way she relates with people. Ask her if you could ever learn from her about how she operates. You might even make a list of questions to ask her.

You may want to find out her philosophies about life and about people. Ask her what inspires her and how she gets by when she's not feeling inspired. Ask her who she learned from and to share some stories of that person with you. Ask her if she can critique your methods and show you ways to improve them. No doubt, you will learn a lot about connecting and about the person you are trying to learn from.

CHAPTER 7

SITUATIONS WHERE CONNECTING ISN'T EASY

I remember in college when I signed up for speech class after a buddy of mine said it would be easy. I took his word and signed up for the class, not knowing that I was in for an eye-opening experience.

The class started out like any other. We were given a schedule and a syllabus, and of course, our first assignment – a five-minute speech about something we were passionate about. That night, I spent a few minutes preparing for the assignment, and closed my books. I was ready. I wasn't worried. How hard could it be to talk for five minutes?

The next day when the teacher called my name, it was my turn to talk. I walked up to the podium and waited for him to give me the go. He looked at me, smiled, and said "begin.". It was game time.

As I stood there waiting for words to come to my mouth, it suddenly felt like the room had fallen silent. I could have heard a pin drop at the other end of the school. My knees began to wobble like loosely placed Jenga bricks.

Finally, I spoke.

My voice cracked and my tone was high pitched. I suddenly realized that I didn't know what to say. I suddenly felt paralyzed with fear. I stood there for about a minute, fidgeting through notecards, sweating, and mumbling incoherent babble that I'm sure left everybody questioning my sanity.

It felt like an eternity, but, it was probably only two or three minutes. Finally, the teacher graciously stepped in, allowing me to take a seat, and sparing us all from enduring any more of the agony.

The teacher's goal was, in a way, to show us how hard it can be to do something as simple as speaking. This thing that comes natural to us when we are with our friends, suddenly becomes so scary and impossible when we are in other settings.

This situation taught me a number of important things. That:

- Some situations require more than we are used to giving.

- Some events go much differently than we imagine they will.

- Some of our confidence can be false – letting us believe we are more prepared for a thing than we really are.

I believe that these lessons apply to us as connectors. Because, as Shakespeare once said, "all of life is a stage." Everywhere we turn, our audience is watching. This is true for that job interview you are nervous about. It's true for Christmas at your mother-in-laws. It's true for that moment when you get on the bus and fifty faces are staring right at you.

The faces change, but the audience is always there. Sometimes, they are hard to win over. Hard to impress or to even get close to. Rarely are they freely giving out their approval and affirmation. You have to earn it, and it's up to you to be confident and prepared.

Since this is what life is so full of, it is of utmost importance that we, as connectors, learn to be better skilled and prepared to handle such situations well. One of the best ways we can prepare ourselves for nearly any difficult situation is by:

#1. TAKING RESPONSIBILITY.

Author, speaker, and businessman, Grant Cardone, says that "there are no tough audiences… just boring speakers." Many of us would like to blame our failures on something other than ourselves, when the failure, most likely, is due to our approach.

When we blame our audience for our failures, we are, in a way, doing to other people what we fear they are doing to us. We are judging them. Even more, we are allowing them to be responsible for our fates, which is almost always a recipe for failure.

Another way we can prepare ourselves for difficult situations is by:

#2. OVERCOMING SHYNESS.

During speech class, something changed in me. I acted differently than I do when I am at home with my family or out with my friends. Something about that situation brought out a characteristic in me that I don't normally see – shyness.

Shyness is something that usually occurs as the result of some underlying fear. When we are afraid of rejection or humiliation. When something threatens our pride, worthiness, or self-esteem, and we take a precautionary measure to save them – we retreat inward.

While shyness is something that results from a desire to seek protection, it usually does more damage than good. It often hurts our chances at connection. It makes us quiet and less confident. It keeps us from being vulnerable in situations where our vulnerability would help a connection form.

Like me, you may not be shy in all situations, but only in some. Perhaps you are bold and confident at home, but reserved and bashful at work. Whether or not you think you are shy, there are probably some ways you could improve.

One thing that can help us is to move towards (rather than away from) those social situations that scare us. Because, our irrational fears tend to decrease when we grow accustomed to what provokes them. If you feel threatened by certain social situations, you should try to become more comfortable around them.

Also, it would do you well to spend more time with people. Being with people will generally make you feel more comfortable with them. In a documentary I recently watched, a cheetah and a golden retriever became best friends. Of course, not because these two species would ever form a friendship out in the wild, but, because they were raised together. They spent time together and grew accustomed to one another, overriding their biological tendencies to fear one another and see each other as different.

Most of our social anxieties and fears would vanish if we just spent more time with other people, rather than imagining the worst-case scenarios about how our interactions with them could go. We would break out of our negative mental cycles, which may be the only place where a real threat exists. As Franklin D. Roosevelt once said, "The only thing we have to fear is fear itself."

In my goal to research and overcome shyness, I have spent a lot of time simply observing people and how they interact. In a recent experience at a coffee shop, I watched two men striking up a conversation.

Apparently, these two men had never met before. One recognized the other as his neighbor, and came over to formally introduce himself. As I watched, I noticed how bold the man was who was taking the initiative to come over. He almost seemed to lack social awareness, charging right into the other man's personal bubble.

But, as they talked, I noticed that they were already becoming acquainted. I saw something good developing, and I began to realize something profound that seemed to go against my logic – that maybe, a bit of obliviousness is just what some situations need. And maybe, what I call politeness and respect of personal space, may really just be a mask that I wear to cover up my insecurities.

If you are someone who struggles with social anxiety, this may be true for you as well. Because, for people like us, a healthy balance involves taking more chances, rather than fewer. It involves simply putting ourselves out there and dwelling less on what could go wrong.

#3. LEARNING TO EXUDE CONFIDENCE.

Another thing I learned from speech class is that my level of confidence changes how others see me. If I'm not sure of myself, it is almost as though I am subliminally telling others that they shouldn't be sure of me either. It is as though I am wearing a great big sign around my neck that says "Needy. Please give me assurance." Some people may stop out of pity, but most people will walk on by.

In fact, I've learned that unconfidence can actually be burdensome to other people. When I don't feel confident, it actually puts a certain amount of pressure on people to make me feel validated – to offer me their assurance, because they can sense that I don't have any.

The funny thing is that people tend to be much more generous with their assurance when they don't feel pressured to give it. It flows from them naturally towards people that make them feel good. The irony here is that we tend to be best at attracting validation when we are least in need of it. Or, when we already have confidence – that's when we aren't sending out silent warning signs that we are dependant.

Perhaps you've noticed how refreshing it can be to talk to somebody who is truly comfortable in her own skin. Something about it is calming. It makes you feel at ease to be yourself, knowing that she isn't depending on you in order to feel sure of herself.

Confidence breeds confidence, and self-uncertainty breeds self-uncertainty. To some degree, people tend to echo back whatever message we are sending them about ourselves. If we want a good response, we have to set the bar by being comfortable and confident first.

One of the best ways we can improve our confidence is by:

#4. BEING PREPARED.

Connection has a lot to do with being prepared. Of course, this isn't to say that you should go out and study each person you plan to encounter and try to predict what they'll say and do. The preparation I'm referring to is more emotional than anything. It means: being prepared to talk to people. To face them. To look them in the eye.

It may involve exercise, getting enough sleep, or mentally rehearsing what we'll say. It could involve positive self-talk or practicing our approach in front of a mirror. It's about doing whatever we have to do in order to feel ready for the day, come what may.

Of course, we can prepare in more specific ways as well. Since you know you are going to meet your cousin today for lunch, it wouldn't hurt to do a little bit of mental homework so that you don't ask questions you've already asked, or tell stories you've already told. Why not spend some time refreshing your memory about the things you talked about last?

If you are going to be in a more formal setting, you may want to practice speaking with a voice recorder. Listening to your recorded voice can be a telling, brutally honest experience. It will give you an objective idea of how you come across to others, which can be extremely useful.

I once did this before a job interview, and I was amazed at how it helped. By gathering my own feedback, I was able to fine-tune my words and hone their delivery, giving a more refined presentation that ended with a job offer.

If you are open to this idea, I recommend it. However, I would also caution you to take your findings with a grain of salt. If you don't like how you sound on a voice recorder, don't let it discourage you. Because, the goal is to become more confident, not more timid.

#5. REALIZING THAT CONNECTING IS NOT ABOUT YOU!

If you look at the source of social anxiety, you see that it usually stems from a fear of what others think of us. Because, we tend to listen poorly when we think we are the focal point of the conversation.

Social anxiety, if you think about it, is a misprioritization of our own needs above others' needs. So, it might relieve us to know that connecting isn't about us. It might help us to know that we don't have to be funny, charming, or interesting. We just have to be interested in other people.

Surprisingly, once we learn to take our focus off of ourselves and place it onto other people, we become much better at connecting, because we are able to care about them, even more than we care about what they think of us.

Do you sometimes feel nervous around people? Do you struggle to know what to say? Try to consider that other people may be feeling the same way. This will get you empathizing with them, which is a great first step in connecting with anyone. It will put you (as well as them) at ease.

Finally, we should note that some of the most difficult relationships to maintain are the ones that we don't think should require maintenance. These are the relationships that we have with our spouses, siblings, kids, and parents. It can be hard to connect with these people – not so much because we fear their rejection, but because we've learned to take our relationships with them for granted.

We have long histories with them and we're confident they'll never leave. We know we don't always have to try so hard, because they'll do most of the work of connecting for us. Whatever the case, we often have low expectations and low energy interactions with these people. So, I have dedicated the next chapter to friendship — a type of relationship that fits into this category. One that, during certain times of our lives, isn't always easy for us to understand and maintain.

CHAPTER 8

CONNECTING WITH FRIENDS

Of all the faces that come and go in our lives, and of all the relationships we have, there is one kind that seems to have a sacred place in our hearts. That is, the kind we have with our friends.

Friends are the ones we often feel closest to. They're the ones we share interests with and have spent large portions of our life with. They are our brothers in arms.

Our partners in crime. They are the ones who have shaped us quite a bit and who we have shaped as well.

Friends are people we care about. We may get angry with them or occasionally lose our patience with them, but above all, our truest, deepest feelings for them are good. We don't want to see our friends suffer. We want them to succeed.

Friendships form in many ways. Sometimes, by birds of a feather tending to flock together. Other times, by opposites attracting. Friendships can form intentionally, by our choosing to associate with somebody because we see they are like us. Or, friendship can evolve by pure chance. A stranger becomes familiar, and out of the blue, you have formed a common bond.

Friendship can make small moments more meaningful. It can make tough times more bearable. As Helen Keller once said, "Walking with a friend in the dark is better than walking alone in the light."

But friendship is ever-changing and it can fluctuate through life's seasons. And, just as friends bring something when they come into our lives, they can take that something away if ever they leave.

And, as we know from our own experiences, this tends to happen as two people go about their lives – sometimes, being changed into different people altogether and losing what they once had in common.

The rules of friendship aren't always self-explanatory, and when we find ourselves in these situations, feeling disconnected from people we once felt close to, it can be confusing. Even, heartbreaking. If we don't know what to make of it, we may find ourselves in despair.

We may take the wrong actions. Or, take none at all, unaware that there may still be things we can do. For this reason, it is worth our while to focus on friendship – how we connect, reconnect, and how we can deal with the feelings that arise whenever friendships come to an end.

When I search my own life for friends to write about, there is one in particular that comes to mind – my lifelong buddy, Scott. Scott and I have known each other since we were three years old. Living next door to one another, we shared backyards. One day, while we were out playing, he came over to my side of the yard and we began to play together.

Later that evening, I came over to his house for tacos. We played toy trains and watched cartoons. Little did either of us know at the time that a lifelong friendship was developing – one that would create many meaningful memories and shape our development for many years.

As we aged, we went to the same schools and even ended up in some of the same classes. We got our driver's licenses at about the same time and went on our first road trips together. We hung out at each others homes, cruised through town together, and flirted with girls together. We went through a lot of the same life events at similar times. When Scott got married, I was his best man. When I got married, he was mine.

However, there were years when it wasn't easy for us to stay close. After high school, Scott moved up to Wisconsin. For the most part, we managed to stay in touch, despite our geographical distance. We'd try to get together on weekends whenever we could – either I'd drive up to his house, or he'd come down to mine.

But one day, it suddenly dawned on me that we had grown apart. During a conversation with him, I realized that a lot of big events had happened in his life that he had never bothered to tell me about. It made me realize that somehow, at some point, I had fallen into a place of less importance in his eyes. I was no longer someone that he reached out to or thought of sharing the details of his life with. This scared me. When did it happen? How?

Sensing the need for repair, I scrambled to give our friendship some attention. I began to make more efforts to call and send him text messages. I even forwarded him a few humorous emails that I thought he would find funny. Sometimes I would make an inside joke about something only he and I understood. But, I was discouraged by his lack of responses. When he did respond, he seemed a bit impersonal and short.

It all made me wonder what was so different in his life that could bring these changes. Had he become too busy? Was life stacking up? Or, had I changed in some way? Had I become weird, uncool, or uninteresting? Did he find a new best friend? My confidence was shaken, and my unnatural attempts reconnect only seemed to be pushing him further away. So, I stopped.

For a long time, I made it a point not to call him – even when I wanted to. Even when there was something that I was dying to tell him about. I kept silent, hoping he would notice his phone wasn't ringing. But, he didn't seem to notice. At least, not like I hoped he would.

In my silence, I felt hurt and angry, and I found myself judging him. "Am I not good enough for him? Is he on some ivory tower, too high and mighty to look down my way?" These judgments gave me a sense of righteousness in my choice to keep distant. But, there was only one problem – they weren't helping. My friend was still growing distant, and it didn't help that I had personal justification.

I began to write my feelings down, which helped me sort out what I was feeling and bring me to a healthier personal place. I finally came to terms with the facts that maybe our friendship just wasn't the same, and maybe it couldn't ever be like it was.

Yet, this realization showed me something else. It let me see our friendship with new eyes. I saw that maybe I had been hindering it by holding on too tightly to the past. After all, if we were different people now, maybe I should stop approaching him as though I know him. Maybe, the past was keeping me from seeing the present.

With that in mind, I decided to make a new attempt to break into his world. I decided to leave the past behind and rewrite my own definition of what it meant to be a friend. I started to ask him more questions about his job and about his kids. I'd call to talk about things that affected him, and mostly, I would let him do the talking. As it turns out, he had a lot to say, and there was a lot I had to learn.

Before long, we had established a new friendship and began to stay connected more frequently. Soon, it no longer felt strange for me to receive a text from him, or for him to receive one from me. We had even circled around back to telling those inside jokes that only he and I knew. Despite all the ways our friendship had changed, in some ways, it hadn't changed at all.

Just a few weeks ago, Scott and I went on a four day kayak trip together in Northern Wisconsin. We had the time of our lives, laughing and sharing stories about our kids, catching smallmouth bass and northern pike, laughing till our sides hurt, and having deep talks about life each night by the glow of a campfire.

It was so great that we decided to make it our new tradition. We plan on going back with his kids, and someday down the road when my girls are old enough, they may come too. Long story short, our friendship was restored. For that, I am very happy.

Through it all, I've learned some valuable lessons. And, a few principles that apply to friendships and relationships in general. The following is a list of those lessons and principles I've learned.

IMPORTANT LESSONS AND PRINCIPLES -

#1. The power of believing -

My friendship with Scott is one that I value. However, this is primarily due to one factor — belief. Since I have always believed in its value, I have continued to pursue it — even when it was difficult and confusing.

As the saying goes, an object is only worth what somebody else is willing to pay for it. When you believe that a relationship has value, you are willing to pay a lot for it with time, intention, and effort. You are willing to invest in it, sacrifice for it, and fight for it.

Belief is important, because we usually find evidence of whatever it is that we believe. If we believe people to be altruistic, good-hearted, or diamonds in the rough, they have a way of proving our suspicions right. Likewise, if we believe they are two-faced, self-centered, or undependable, they will also prove our suspicions right.

The funny irony is that we tend to get out of relationships whatever we believe we will. So, we might as well believe the best we can. If we look for evidence of good things, chances are, we will find it. If we find it, chances are, our actions will reflect it, and we'll begin to treat the relationship with more care.

#2. The power of suggestion -

When we were younger, Scott once told me that we were best friends. Because of this, my mind opened up to the idea, and I began to hold our friendship in even higher regard. This, I believe, is an example of how the power of suggestion can impact our relationships.

As creatures geared for survival, our minds are always working. In order to lessen that workload, we often rely on the work others have already done. We look to our friends to tell us which shows we should watch, and our parents to tell us which foods are healthy. We rely on people to tell us what is or isn't worth talking about, and what does or doesn't have value – including our relationships.

We rely on suggestions. We can use suggestions in our relationships to get others on the same page with us, just as Scott did with me. You know that special thing that exists between you and your mom, your niece, or your old friend from high school? Do you want these people to see what you see? Suggest it. Once you do, you increase the odds that others will follow suit and adopt your point of view.

Many of the suggestions we make are subtle. Simply by going up to somebody and saying hello, you are indirectly suggesting to him that you think he is worth saying hello to. If you reach to shake his hand, you are suggesting that you respect him enough to want his handshake.

Similarly, you are also suggesting something about yourself. You are saying that you deem yourself worthy of that person's handshake, attention, and reciprocation. When Scott told me that we were best friends, he was suggesting something to me about himself – that he saw himself as a best friend, and that I could think of him the same way.

Suggestion is a powerful thing, but we should note that there is another side to it. Because, even our inactions are full of suggestions. By choosing not to go up to a person and say hello, or reach over for a handshake, or offer a smile and start up a conversation, we are likewise suggesting that there is a valid reason why we haven't done so.

Our inactions suggest that certain actions aren't worth our taking, and therefore, aren't worth anyone else's taking either. By not making a move, we can greatly lessen the chances that others will make a move towards connection with us or even see the value in doing so.

Remember the power of suggestion and how it is impacting our relationships all the time – even in the subtlest of ways!

#3. The power of association -

The power of association has to do with the way that we become like those we spend time with. I spent a lot of time with Scott during my formative years and became a lot like him. I formed interests, attitudes, tastes, and habits that were similar to his – all because of the power of association.

But at the same time, he was becoming like me. I transmitted many of my own characteristics to him as well. What does this mean for us as connectors? That, in a way, people are like mirrors. If we want to see good reflections in them, we should give them something good to reflect.

If we want them to be welcoming, we ourselves should be welcoming. If we want them to be agreeable, we ourselves should be agreeable. We can inspire people to be confident, well-mannered, accepting, and outgoing, simply by exhibiting these characteristics ourselves.

This is especially helpful in those tough situations where we find it difficult to relate with a certain person. Rather than blindly hoping that person will be a good connector, we ourselves can take the lead, and there is a great chance that they will follow.

#4. The power of expression -

As the common saying goes, it's not what you say; it's how you say it. As it turns out, this statement is scientifically correct. Relationships expert, John

Gottman, talks about the ability to predict how well a conversation will go, simply by how it starts. Basically, if a person starts a conversation using a soft voice, a gentle tone, and a tactful word choice, he is 96% more likely to have a productive conversation.

When I think of how this applies to my friendship with Scott, I realize that most of our interactions in life have started out well. Whenever it had been a while since we'd seen each other, we always greeted each other with big smiles, a handshake, and a bear hug. This, I believe, has always played a big role in how well we got along.

We all tend to notice other people's' reactions towards our presence. And, there is a big difference between people who greet us with a frown and people who greet us with a smile. When you walk in your front door and your dog is wagging his tail, barking and jumping around in circles, his enthusiasm is contagious. You might fall to the ground and start making a commotion yourself.

Can you think of how you come across to other people? Are your shoulders slouched or are they upright? Do you look bored, or do you look like you really want to be there? All of this plays a large role in how your meetings with people will go.

If we can convey a certain amount of affection and excitement for others, it goes a long way to set the tone for how our interactions with them carry on.

#5. The power of respecting boundaries -

In my attempts to reconnect with Scott, I often found myself unsure of the right direction forward. I usually wanted to pick things up right where we had left off, but the truth was that we were no longer close. So, I had to approach our friendship with consideration to the fact that it had changed.

The result? I was eventually allowed back into a deeper personal space of his, but only because I proved myself trustworthy with the small amounts of space he gave me. Little by little, I reestablished my trust and familiarity with him. In short, I respected his boundaries.

As humans, we all have boundaries. For some people, we will lower our guard walls down – usually, to the degree we know and trust them. Your spouse shares a room and a bed with you, and is allowed to know your thoughts, emotions, and plans. Your best friend is allowed to know where you stand on matters of faith and politics, which are things you wouldn't share with just anyone.

However, human boundaries seem to be ever-changing. Just as one person may have been allowed access to your personal space at one time, he may be denied access to that space at another time – especially if something has been done to change the levels of familiarity, trust, or respect between you.

As connectors, we must keep this in mind, because we are attempting to break into other people's worlds. It is important that we do so with respect and consideration to where we stand among the people we are trying to get to know.

We should take the amount of space they give us. No more. No less. If we do not abuse it, the common result is that they will give us more. If we do abuse it, prying too much into their personal lives, judging them, or pushing them to do something they're not comfortable with, the common result is that they will regret giving us any.

There is generally a certain amount of space that we always have access to. With the rare exception that someone has a restraining order against you, you can go up and say hello or offer a friendly smile to just about anyone. You don't need permission to give a handshake or talk about the weather. These simple things can always be done and they are effective ways of breaking into people's worlds.

#6. Restrategizing your technique -

In my attempts to reconnect with Scott, I wrote down a lot of my thoughts and feelings on paper. At one point, I actually considered sharing those thoughts with him in the form of a letter. In hindsight, I am very glad that I didn't.

I realize now that it probably would have only confused the situation. And, it would have been a bad way of trying to start a conversation with someone that I was already unlikely to talk to. My letter was helpful for only one person – me. It helped me understand my own feelings. It gave me the clarity I needed. But, it's not what Scott needed. He needed me to take a different approach to being a friend.

Sometimes, when we feel like a friendship is over, we get too caught up trying to figure out how it ended. But, our time would be much better spent looking at how friendships begin, rather than how they end. Not only is this easier to wrap our heads around, it serves a more productive purpose. Because, if it's true that we can cause friendships to fail by taking the wrong actions, it should also be true that we can make them grow by taking the right actions. What are those right actions? To see them, simply look at how new friends think and behave towards each other.

New friends typically are very accepting and inviting. They try to know, understand, and meet each other's needs. They are good listeners and encouragers, and they typically give one another the benefit of the doubt. They look for the truth in what the other is saying. They are quick to say I'm sorry and quick to forgive, just to name a few.

But, to make these habits and mindsets more applicable, I have broken them down into ten main categories which we can focus on and apply if we want to see our own friendships improving. If we do this, we will be taking our focus away from the problem and placing it on the solution.

1. Be a Builder.

Have a constructive mindset toward the relationship.

2. Be agreeable.

Look for the truth in what the other person is saying.

3. Be a listener.

Be curious about the other person and interested in what he says, thinks, and feels.

4. Be an empathizer.

Try to relate with the person and put yourself in his/her shoes.

5. Be responsible.

Own up to your mistakes. Say "I'm sorry" quickly, should you in any way step out of line.

6. Be thick-skinned.

Try not to be hurt too easily, or to set unreasonable expectations in a person.

7. Be intuitive.

Try to be sensitive to a person's needs, likes, and dislikes.

8. Be courteous.

Remember the golden rule. Treat others the way that you would like to be treated.

9. Be an encourager.

Be positive and uplifting towards the other. Offer compliments and encouragement.

10. Be gracious.

Extend the benefit of the doubt. Try to believe the best you can about a person's actions and intentions.

Basically, we should keep doing whatever we once did that made our friendships grow and thrive. If we become too complacent (as many of us do), we will probably find ourselves wondering why our friendships aren't what they could (or used to) be.

Taking small steps to improve will not only help rebuild your friendships, it will also give you a sense of control in them. You are doing something positive and constructive about a known problem in your life, which can be very liberating.

Lastly, keep in mind that friendship is a fairly broad term. One definition of the word, "Friend," is: "the opposite of an enemy." So, this means that your dad is your friend. Your aunt Judy is your friend. Your grandmother is your friend. And, it means you can use these friendship building principles to strengthen all kinds of relationships – even those that you wouldn't classify as friendships.

DETERMINING IF A FRIENDSHIP IS SAVABLE/WORTH SAVING -

We've spent some time talking about old friendships and what we can do to restore them. But, before moving on, there is something we should stop and ask ourselves: "Should we?" In other words, are all relationships worth our rebuilding?

You've long been thinking about your old friend. Some of the best times you ever had were spent with... wait... what's his name again? It'll come to you eventually, because he was really a great guy. Or, could it be that he's not really what you're missing?

Maybe, what you really miss isn't a person at all, but a certain season of your life. You miss the way it felt to be seventeen and single with nothing but time. That old friend of yours is just a symbol of that time. A person who, for whatever reason, you associate it with. This would be good to know before you pick up the phone. Becoming clear about your sentiments would be a good place to start. On that note, there are a few other things you may want to consider.

You may want to ask yourself if that old friend is even the same person you knew back then. Because, people change. Chances are, you may not even be the same person you used to be. Neither of you may share any of the things that you once had in common. Is that going to be an issue? Maybe, maybe not. But, it's at least worth thinking about.

After all, you only have so much precious time and energy to invest in your connections. How much of it do you want to give to a relationship that might not benefit you or anyone else? Since life is so full, we have to choose our relationships carefully. Each time we do, we choose them over something else. Which relationships are worth your time?

Finally, you should ask yourself if the relationship you want to rebuild was ever even good for you. Maybe, upon further consideration, you'll realize that the person you're thinking of was a bad influence on you in some way. Maybe he didn't make you feel respected and had a habit of putting his own interests first. Maybe, you always wanted him to like you, but he never valued your relationship the way that you did. These are all valid things to consider.

Once we have considered all of these questions, and if we have decided that we DO in fact want to restore an old bond, we can then start trying to get that old friendship ball rolling. However, we must remember that success is never guaranteed. Even if we have all the best intentions and motives, our best efforts still might not get us what we're after.

Ultimately, the person you want to reconnect with will have to desire a reconnection with you. As the saying goes, it always "takes two to tango." And, sometimes we find that the person we want to dance with does not feel like dancing. This subject, we will talk about next.

DEALING WITH LOSS -

I should mention that when I was trying to reacquaint with Scott, I was also trying to reacquaint with a lot of other old friends. I happened to be going through a major life transition at the time – living in a new state and feeling like a total outsider. It greatly magnified those feelings of hurt and frustration that I had felt in my friendships.

As a newcomer in a new area, I often felt timid and shy in my new surroundings – at work, at church, and in my neighborhood. I didn't know what to make of my emotions and often felt embarrassed for even having them. Why was all of this stuff affecting me so much? Why couldn't I just shake it off?

Until then, I had always looked down on people in this situation. I thought that they were just whiners or pansies who didn't know how to pick up a phone, lacking the willpower or the gumption to take control of their own fates. Now, I was one of these people, discovering that I might not have all the answers after all.

I was also discovering that I wasn't bulletproof, and that small things could totally trigger my insecurities. I found that I can actually be pretty touchy and sensitive whenever a friend didn't return a phone call or a text. Such small things could immediately make me defensive and doubtful of the good in people.

At times, I even found myself playing games with certain people, ignoring those who I had felt ignored by — trying to inflict the same type of pain on them that I felt they had caused me. In retrospect, I always realized that these reactions were immature... especially when I would discover later that most people had valid reasons for not responding. Every time I thought their silence had something to do with me, it didn't.

The real problem, in the end, had to do with my own unanswered questions about my worth. My own fears, insecurities, and baggage. This is what kept me seeing reality through a distorted lens, assuming and exaggerating things out of proportion, and thinking that my likability as a person was always on the line.

These doubts affected every part of me – even my ability to connect with others. They could usually sense my touchiness and guardedness, and they saw it as a red flag. If anything, I was giving them reason to keep their distance. The irony of it all was that I tended to chase good connections away right when I was most hurting from a lack of them.

Fortunately, these experiences have led me to discover some very solid truths. The first is: You can't always trust your emotions. Sometimes, there are just too many unseen factors playing a role, and it's almost impossible to stay objective.

I've learned that a bad day at work can easily follow me home. An argument with my wife can make me unknowingly edgy and needy for validation. Rejection from one place in life can cross over into another, making me scarily susceptible to being injured by the slightest touch. And, being wrong about who is to blame.

I've also learned that not all relationships can be saved. While I was able to reconnect with Scott, there were many other friends I tried reaching out to that I wasn't able to reconnect with. Sometimes, there are just too many hindering factors — seen and unseen.

The only constant variable in relationships may be the fact that they change. People change. While some people may walk away with hard feelings, most of them walk away simply because life is pulling them in some other direction.

Friendships that end usually end without explanation. Nor, a formal goodbye. If anything, people usually plan on staying in touch, but fail to. As time goes on, life pushes certain relationships out of sight and out of mind, until one day, people we once saw as friends, we now see as strangers.

When we find ourselves here, it usually doesn't make sense to our hearts. We often feel hurt or abandoned or betrayed by it, when really, no such thing has happened. We may long for an explanation, but we rarely get one. At least, none that satisfy us. Partially, because no one is able to explain it; partially because even if they could, they've drifted from our lives.

What we do with our uncertainty determines everything about how we will move on as individuals. If we are able to keep believing the best about people, we will be far better off, reaching conclusions that help us understand life, people, and ourselves.

Loss is part of the human experience, and it is okay to mourn when we experience it. It does not make us any stronger or better off to deny the pain's realness or the fact that it affects us deeply.

Our pursuit, in the end, should be to seek wholeness, and to keep from letting our hurts change us into something we are not. This can make us more likely to improve future connections and maintain the ones we still have.

When we find ourselves hurting, acting immaturely, or feeling tempted to believe the worst about people, it is usually a sign that we should stop looking outside ourselves and start looking within. Chances are, there is something in us that we need to stop and address.

DEALING WITH REJECTION -

At the start of my junior year, I attended a new high school. From the very first day, it felt like my presence was totally unwelcome. I was called names, pushed around, and laughed at. I was shunned and picked on in the hallways. Once, I even had to run for my life.

At the time. I suspected that it all said something about me. I didn't know why else I could be so hated, other than that there must have been something wrong with me. I believed there must have been some defect or obvious flaw in me that everyone else could see but me.

Of course, that wasn't true. And, time would show me. I would eventually see that none of this was my fault. I never asked to be taunted. I never instigated feuds or invited hostility. I was picked on simply because a few unhappy people needed something else to focus on than the one thing they hated even more than me – themselves.

I couldn't please them. Nor could I change them. Nothing in my power could fix whatever it was that was going on in them. I realized that there are simply people in life who are always searching for someone to feel bigger than, because, deep inside, they feel small.

Such people, I've found, are everywhere; not just in high school. Even once you've graduated and gone out into the working world, they're still there – wearing different faces, perhaps, but, they are the same at heart.

This is the pain of rejection. It's when people make it clear that they don't like us. They may say they hate us. Or, they may just act like it. When we experience it, it's hard not to believe that it says something about us as people. Hard not to believe that we are failures or losers.

In fact, it is especially hard when we are rejected – not by strangers, but by the ones we know and love. The people we have been close to – who, in fact, still have a close enough place in our hearts to wound us significantly.

It is a cold, sharp dagger when you find that your old best friend no longer looks your way when you cross paths, or when she ignores your phone calls and texts. You once did everything together. You once shared secrets and experiences and believed you always be a part of each other's lives.

It's hard to heal when a family member makes you feel like you're not important. Perhaps, in subtle ways, he lets everyone else know that they are special except for you. Or, in more blatant ways. He tells you to your face that you aren't wanted.

The message of rejection is always that there is something wrong with you. You aren't valuable. You aren't likable. You don't belong. And, it is a message that is always untrue. It doesn't reflect you; it reflects the perspective of the people giving it.

Yet, however untrue that message may be, we should acknowledge that it always hurts to receive it. The fact that it is invalid or that we don't deserve it never seems to subtract from the fact that our hearts have been scarred and have some mending to do.

Rejection is something that we sometimes can't escape in life. And, when we find ourselves facing it, there is no simple solution. Usually, we are left with nothing but a choice to press on. And, to change. If we're wise, we will begin to look for new people to surround ourselves with. People who believe in us and who help us believe in ourselves.

If you can relate with any of this, I may be able to recommend a few resources. One is called: When Friendship Hurts, by Jan Yager. It deals with the painful side of friendship and the many encompassing feelings of betrayal, abandonment, and self-doubt that we can feel in life's changing relational tides.

Another great book called Rejection Proof, by Jia Jiang, talks about dealing with the pain of rejection and learning to overcome it. It builds an understanding of the threat of rejection, and how our fear of the threat is often worse than the threat itself.

One more, is a great book by Eric Greitens, called Resilience. This book goes into depth on the subject of feeling discouraged by life and the temptation to stay down after a fall.

CONNECTION AND CONFLICT -

Of course, what may feel like rejection, may simply be conflict. Conflict can present with a lot of the same symptoms as rejection, but it is fundamentally much different. And, more curable.

Unlike rejection, conflict doesn't mean that someone dislikes you. It doesn't mean you are unwanted, unvalued, or thought less of. It just means that, for some reason, a rift has developed in the relationship, causing it not to function as it should. Most likely, due to unsettled differences.

Conflict usually means that two people simply aren't seeing eye to eye. Maybe there is an issue that has surfaced and needs to be addressed. Someone has been unfair. Someone has not been doing their part. Certain expectations, responsibilities, or perspectives are in dispute, and it has reached a point in the relationship where it can no longer be ignored.

Here, both involved parties usually feel a certain amount of discomfort. And, they are confronted with a choice about how they will proceed. They may choose to ignore the fact that they cannot see eye to eye. They may choose to discuss their differences and work for a compromise. Or, they may choose to part ways, being that they see no way around the conflict.

Conflict is something that can occur in nearly all relationships, regardless of the type. It can happen among spouses, dating couples, business partners, and best friends. It can happen among people who have nothing in common. Or, people who think they have everything in common. Despite whatever common grounds that are lacked or shared, disagreements inevitably arise. Over time, if not solved, they hinder the growth and functionality of a relationship.

Conflict can be uncomfortable. It can make a relationship feel as though it is being tested. And, in a sense, it is. Much like a muscle that is being stretched during exercise, our relationships become stretched during conflict. And, they tend to either be broken by the stretching, or, made stronger.

In most cases, it is best to address whatever is causing the conflict. While this may be uncomfortable, it often leads people to a better understanding of each other. And, it leads them to become more accepting of each other's differences. When compromise is possible, it is usually the best solution.

However, it may not always be possible to reach a compromise. In many cases, people just have different core beliefs and they never will agree on a middle place to meet in. They must simply learn to coexist. This is where the popular phrase comes from, "Agree to disagree."

If we cannot work through conflict, it usually is not because of our differences; it has to do with our level of willingness to respect and live with those differences. In most cases, when relationships diverge, it is because two people did not want to make it work.

The important thing is to recognize conflict for what it is and to keep from assuming that it is more. It is not an omen of a relationship ending. It is not the implication of a flaw in either person, or a sign that you, as a person, are not accepted by somebody else. It is simply a sign that something in your relationship needs attention.

If you would like to learn how to grow through conflict in your relationships, there are many great resources that are available. Crucial Conversations, by Kerry Patterson, is an excellent book that talks about handling tough discussions when stakes and emotions are high. Or, John Gottman's "Why Marriages Succeed or Fail" is a great book, also discussing what conflict is and how it can be dealt with.

Chances are, all of our relationships would improve if we simply took the time to learn some simple conflict-resolution skills, and made it a practice of ours to apply them at the earliest signs of discord. For now, I have listed a few helpful, simple conflict-resolution principles. They are:

1. Avoid making negative assumptions about the other person.

2. Avoid attacking his/her character.

3. Avoid using "you statements" when addressing matters between you.

4. Apologize as quickly as possible for mistakes you have made.

5. Be a good listener.

If you find that you are in conflict with somebody you care about, don't panic. Remember that it doesn't mean the end is near. In fact, if you learn to handle your conflict well, the proverbial "bump in the road" can actually be something that lifts your relationship up off the ground!

CHAPTER 9

CARING FOR YOURSELF

If you've ever flown in a plane, then you know that in the event of an emergency, the flight-attendant will instruct you to attach your own oxygen mask before helping others attach theirs. This is because, you will not be able to help anyone if you yourself are lying on the floor, passed out due to a lack of oxygen.

In relationships, a similar concept applies. That is, if we aren't taking care of ourselves, or if our core needs aren't being met, we tend to be poor connectors. We become needy, which keeps us focused only on the taking elements of friendship, rather than the giving aspects, and the balance of a healthy relationship is thrown off.

Not long ago, I experienced my own relationships suffering due to a neglect of certain basic needs. Shortly after my daughter was born, my wife and I spent many hours in bed, staring at the ceiling. My daughter would wake us up every few hours, and we were often unable to fall back to sleep.

As this carried on for a matter of months, I tried the "fake it till I make it" approach, hoping that no one would notice how fatigued I was, as long as I was smiling. But, I soon found that no amount of faking it could spare me from the negative effects of sleep-deprivation. My attention span and short term memory were suffering. My reactions to people became half-hearted and sluggish.

Sometimes, during the day, I almost felt like I was sleepwalking. People would talk to me, but it was like I was watching their lips move and as though I couldn't really hear what they were saying. I would nod, smile, and go through the motions, but I was only acting. Eventually, my apathy showed through.

During this time, a lot of my relationships suffered. Because, I found that I didn't make a very good friend when I was acting like a zombie – unable to focus, listen, or give any of my attention to anyone else's cares and concerns. My own needs were so neglected that I lacked the capacity to see the needs of others.

I know that such circumstances are sometimes inevitable. I know that there are times in life when we go through phases where more is demanded of us, and we feel like we are being stretched past our limits. When a baby is born. When there is unresolved tension in a relationship. When you get laid off, lose a loved one, or face some other major life transition, it is normal to endure a certain amount of time that is both trying and confusing. However, it becomes abnormal and damaging if that it is prolonged, and if exhaustion becomes a common fixture in your life.

Did you know? Sleep debt is considered going more than two consecutive nights with less than seven full hours of sleep per night. Wow. This is convicting. If it's true, it means that I've been in sleep debt my entire life. So has nearly everyone I've ever known.

One problem is that we tend to look at ourselves as an exception to the rules of self-care. At some level, we believe we can avoid the repercussions that everyone else is subject to. And yet, it's so common to find people who aren't the exception... people who are drained, depressed, stressed, and burnt out, thinking that they don't have time to slow down for themselves.

We should seriously consider how this takes its toll on our well-being – physically, emotionally, and mentally. No one is immune, no matter how tough we think we are. And, we should realize the significance that this has on our connections. Because, this burnt-out place is usually where isolation begins. And, so many other things, such as addiction, unhealthy habits, and unhelpful coping mechanisms.

Personally, I've found that when I am struggling to relate with people, the problem is in me; not them. In fact, whenever I start to feel like the world is ganging up in me, I've come to see it as a warning sign that something big is going on in me – something that I need to stop and deal with.

Personal wellness isn't a luxury, or a thing that only selfish people have time for. Let go of this notion, if you're tempted to believe it. Surely, there will always be people who don't make time for themselves, and who see you as selfish for taking care of yourself. Don't worry. You'll be the one helping them find their oxygen mask when you're the only one who's still able to breathe.

Give yourself the attention you need. You don't need someone else's permission. You aren't silly for recognizing your own needs either, so, don't let anyone guilt you into ignoring something so crucial.

If you are the type of person to ignore your own needs, there are a few simple, effective steps that will benefit your wellness, and ultimately, the health of your relationships. They aren't rocket-science, and you've probably heard them before. But, try to think of them, not as "old news," but as things you can start doing to charge your relational batteries. They are:

- Maintain a consistent sleep schedule.

- Maintain a healthy (and consistent) diet.

- Exercise regularly.

- Get help from an outside source – a mentor, a counselor, or a life-coach.

- If necessary, join a support group for any addictions, or to deal with any emotionally traumatic situations.

- Keep up with practical matters – they can easily become emotional matters. Clutter, unfinished task lists, financial problems, and physical health concerns can deteriorate your emotional well-being, making you less equipped to be a good father, friend, spouse, or employee.

Again, none of this is rocket-science, but it's stuff that we neglect on a regular basis, and therefore, stuff that warrants repeating. When we work on ourselves, we are indirectly working on our relationships. The better self-maintainers we are, the better connectors we make.

CHAPTER 10

BEING THE CHANGE THAT YOU WANT TO SEE -

LEADING BY EXAMPLE

It has been said that we should "be the change we want to see." If we want to see a more peaceful world… if we want to see less poverty… If we want to see more kindness and compassion, then we ourselves should be the ones to bring about such changes, rather than hope that others bring the changes we would like to see.

One of the most powerful types of persuasion is the kind that leads by example. This is simply because we live in a world that is full of hypocrites and bad examples. Our hearts grow weary in search of authentic leaders. Occasionally, however, we are stirred awake by those rare people who take initiative and who practice what they preach. If you're unsure how to get there, start by thinking about your own desires.

You probably like the way it feels when your own telephone rings, or when you can tell that a friend genuinely wants to hear the sound of your voice. Or, when you have some big news that you want to share, and someone you care about is truly interested in hearing it. If so, it all goes to prove one main thing – that you fully understand how much you can be offering to other people simply by doing these same things for them – things that you wish they were doing for you.

We all have to unlearn some of our bad, selfish habits of waiting for others to make the first move. If we take the initiative to be good connectors ourselves, we will probably find more people flocking to us than we know what to do with.

Another way we can make ourselves into good connectors is by being authentic. People sense if we aren't really interested in them, just as they sense that a suspicious email from the Prince of South Africa isn't really worth $250,000.

With all the spam, false advertising, and clickbait that we're subjected to nowaday, never before has it been so important for us to be real with people. Leading by example means actually caring about other people — not just pretending to.

If you don't wonder how your friend is handling his divorce, then maybe it's time to become curious. If you don't think about your niece's ambition to become a great soccer player, then it's time to start. Once you become interested, you'll find how little effort connecting can be. Because, when you're truly interested in people, they are automatically drawn toward you. They will have more reasons than not to desire your company and influence.

CHANGE YOUR ENVIRONMENT -

One of the best ways to achieve some of these changes is by changing our environments. A lot of us don't spend time with people who strengthen us or challenge us to be better people. If we did, we would see a lot of growth happening without much effort.

The power of environment is strong. If you question this, just think for a moment about the weather. Can you deny that it affects you? No one who is in the sun can say that he chooses not to be affected by it. Nor can anyone choose not to be affected by his environment.

Our environments dictate a lot of things – not just where we spend our time, but who we spend it with. This is why our work environments have such a large bearing on us – our moods and perspectives.

Outside of work, it is also important who we choose to spend our time with. We can expect to be shaped by the company we choose, as well as by the places we inhabit. If either of these is toxic, it would be in our interest to search for new places and people to be around.

Alcoholics know to stay away from bars and gamblers know to stay away from casinos. For those of us who want to be better connectors (or who know that our struggle lies in making/maintaining connections), it would serve us well to stop spending in ways that are damaging to our connections.

We may even want to consider another place of employment. That is, if the one we're at is only filling our accounts, but draining us empty in every other conceivable way. Money may not be the only determining factor after all.

Finally, consider that we may be bringing our bad environments with us. These days, our smartphones and digital devices are our tagalong distractions, keeping us locked up and unreachable wherever we go. Those tiny little earbuds that we jam in our ears are sending a signal inward, but they also are sending a message outward to the rest of the world, saying, "Stay away. I'm preoccupied. Don't invade my personal bubble."

All in all, it would help us to consider these factors, and to keep an open eye out for any opportunities we have to upgrade our environments.

CONCLUSION

As I think about how I would like to conclude this book, a certain quote comes to mind;

"No man is an island,

Entire of itself,

Every man is a piece of the continent,

A part of the main..."

- John Donne.

When I first read this statement, it made me envision humanity as a single entity – one that each person is an integral part of. It struck me as a cool concept – one that I enjoyed imagining. But, I soon realized that it didn't seem true. At least, not always. Not for everyone.

Many of us, despite our membership to the human race, feel an overwhelming lack of connection and belonging in our lives. No, we may not be islands, but let's face it… there sure does seem to be an awful lot of water between us and those other specks of land.

But, what if we do have more in common with the rest of the world than we realize? What if we aren't as isolated as we sometimes feel? What if, beneath these waves, we are connected somewhere deep down? Sure, it's a tough concept to consider; but many true concepts are.

Perhaps, this is a truth we can only come to know through trust and experience. And, by taking a few positive actions, such as:

Giving up false familiarity. Letting go of guilt. Choosing not to wait for inspiration. Turning off our mental autopilots. Being stronger than our own shyness, fear, and temptations to act invulnerable. Resolving our inner personal matters and taking care of our own deep needs. Restrategizing our techniques. Showing up. Offering our presence, both physically and emotionally. Lending a helping hand. Speaking positive truths. Recognizing special opportunities that are all around us and learning to seize them while they're there. Building up our own levels of confidence and preparedness. Learning to be effective listeners. Learning to relate to people in their way and in their timing. And, learning to give our relationships what they need — effort, intention, consistency, and time.

If we do these things, we may find the proverbial landmass that John Donne is referring to – that place that all men are a part of. The one that joins us all together beneath life's visible waters, no matter how deep; no matter how wavy at the surface.

As we grow closer to experiencing greater connection, the greater our sense of belonging will be in this world. And, the more we will experience depth and meaning in our lives. Because, while life is about many things, it is mostly about who we share it with. People are what matter. The time we spend strengthening our bonds with them is, perhaps, the best investment we can make.

THE END

Dear reader,

If you have any questions, comments or concerns, feel free to email me at Newbooksforyou@Hotmail.com. Please mention if you'd like to be on the mailing list too, so that you'll stay updated with free book offers as new books are released. If you'd like to see which other books and products I have to offer, please visit www.Authorcaleb.com.

Please take a moment to review this book. Remember that writers need YOUR help in order to stay writing (and in order to stay growing). Thanks so much for your time, support and interest.

Sincerely,

C J Kruse

ALL BOOKS BY C J KRUSE:

How To Stop Arguing: A guide on breaking argumentative cycles in relationships.

Marriage Is Work: A practical manual for married couples who want to make their marriages better.

10 Ways To Make Sure You Never Stop Being Defensive: A book about overcoming defensiveness.

Meeting Rich: A true story about the last 3 weeks of Rich Mullins life.

The 28 Day Marriage Challenge: A one-month Christian-based marriage calendar for couples.

10 Ways To Make Sure You Never Find Happiness: A book about Happiness, and how (not) to find it.

To Blame A Sunset: An introspective book about life's emptiness and how to live with it.

Made in the USA
Middletown, DE
31 July 2019